An
OLD LION
ROARS *At*
DEMENTIA

J. Stewart Schneider, J.D.

An
OLD LION
ROARS *At*
DEMENTIA

CITI OF
BOOKS

CITIOFBOOKS, INC.
3736 Eubank NE Suite A1
Albuquerque, NM 871113579
www.citiofbooks.com
Hotline: 1 (877) 3892759
Fax: 1 (505) 9307244

Ordering Information:

Quantity sales. Special discounts are available on quantity purchases by corporations, associations, and others. For details, contact the publisher at the address above.

Printed in the United States of America.

ISBN13:   Softcover   979-8-89391-413-9
                    eBook   979-8-89391-414-6

Library of Congress Control Number: 2024922223

Table of Contents

Here's Why

During my long life, I have been a successful politician, an unsuccessful politician, a police dispatcher, a cop, a radio host, a felony prosecutor, a published technical writer, a computer programmer, a performance musician and recording artist, a Christian minister, and, at various times, a bread truck driver and a door-to-door salesman. For the past 15 years or so I've served a Presbyterian Church as their "stated supply speaker" although I am not a Presbyterian. (My ministerial credentials are with the Christian Church, Disciples of Christ). That's a lot.

Most recently, I have been diagnosed with "vascular dementia", described as

> **Dementia caused by problems in the supply of blood to the brain, typically a series of minor strokes, leading to worsening cognitive abilities, the decline occurring step by step.**

The literature continues, dryly, to state

> **People with vascular dementia present with progressive cognitive impairment, frequently step-wise, after multiple cerebrovascular events (strokes). Some people may appear to improve between events and decline after further silent strokes. A rapidly deteriorating condition may lead to death from a stroke, heart disease, or infection.**

Finally, we are told that the prognosis is "poor".

We arrive in this world as a blank slate. Gradually, very gradually, we come to perceive our wider world, beginning with our immediate surroundings. Searching for a metaphor, I struck on a Ferris Wheel. One enters the Ferris Wheel at its lowest point, a perspective from which only the nearest and clearest things about the environment can be seen. Then, with no effort, the Wheel begins to rotate, drawing us backward and upward. We cannot see where we are going, only where we have been, and we have no idea of the force which is driving us in so singular a fashion.

Nonetheless, we rise higher and as we do so, our range of perception increases. Now we see over the tops of buildings. We can scan the horizon. We begin to see the connections which knit our world into a whole, the streets and the electric wires, other people strolling, people previously unknown to us. As we move ever higher into the unknown, we are positioned to see more of our world until at last we reach the very top where the Wheel stops, leaving us rocking gently, surveying the entirety of the world available to us. From here, we are masters of all which is granted to us. From here, all mysteries open to us are revealed and we revel in the glory of it all.

But such elation does not last. The Wheel begins again its slow rotation so that we are forced to observe our decline as the world and its connections slowly slip from our grasp. Inevitably, we will return to the point of loss of perception, loss of understanding, again the state of helplessness from which we began. It's well and good to counsel me to enjoy the view while I have it, but the inevitability of this loss of autonomy preys upon me. Lions roar to announce their presence and to boast of their strength. Old lions roar from nostalgia and frustration. This little book represents my reflections on what I have seen as I look back on it from my current, more enfeebled, state as well as my thoughts on the world I now inhabit illuminated by the world as I remember it.

When I ask why I would do such a thing as to write a book, my mind brings up thoughts of my father's coffin. In my mind's eye,

Dad's coffin has been stuffed with paper, each sheet representing a success or a failure, a distressing moment or a celebratory one. Things that bothered Dad were carefully noted as were those joys he experienced. His time in the Philippines during World War II was thoroughly documented as was his joyous return to the states. All of it, the good, the bad and the ugly, was stuffed tightly into his coffin, then the lid was screwed on tight. None of it would ever again trouble a living soul once Dad and his memories were filed away beneath the sod, but none of it would ever again be celebrated, either. Like the genealogical studies I dabble in, each life is reduced to name, date of birth, date of death. What a heresy to something so precious as a human life! We insist that Dad's experiences were enough for one lifetime but insufficient for anything more, so they should lie undisturbed and unacknowledged. And yet…

What a gift a human life is. What a messy, happy, chaotic thing! The elation! The sorrow of loss! The errors from which he learned! It is a treasury beyond price, yet at its end we file it all away and reduce that life to only a name and the space of time during which the adventure played out.

John Franklin Schneider

February 23,1917
October 23, 2006

Can we not do better? Can we not find a way to treasure the inestimable adventure that is a human life? Hence, this book. I will roar and perhaps the sound of it will speak to the future of my children.

When I was a young man, I walked a mental path of smooth macadam with few, if any, tripping hazards. I didn't stride, for I have never been that confident, but I walked upright, admiring my surroundings. Every thought which entered my consciousness brought with it a legion of other, connected, memories so that my mental environment was a place of wondrous variety.

Then came age and vascular dementia. Now, my mental environment is sparse, more empty and unremarkable. No more does one thought summon others. No more am I reminded of pleasanter times by some passing vision. If I am to speak, I must speak now.

What I wish is that inner peace could be summoned by an act of will, yet I have not the talent. The best that I can do is to find compromise between the forces to which I am in thrall and my world as I remember it. I will make those compromises, but I will also embrace my anger! I will not go quietly into that good night. I will roar!

A Bird on the Wire

I took the garbage out after supper. As I returned to the front porch, I heard birdsong and thought I might sit and listen. I don't have the first idea why I did that. Birds don't interest me and neither does birdsong but this little guy was making himself known. I think it was a robin, but he was too far away to be sure. There he sat, on my electric wire, singing his heart out. I relaxed into the chair and just listened, feeling kinship with him.

Any ornithologist would tell me that he was announcing his availability to any lonely females in the area, but there were plainly none about. There were two male Cardinals who were performing aerial acrobatics of eye-popping complexity, but they were doing so silently. It was not for them that the Robin sang. Nor was it for me. Ornithologists or no ornithologists, it is my belief that he sang to announce his presence to the world. "Here I am, in my weakness and my strength, in my short life, I am here."

Do we not all, from time to time, need to announce ourselves? Is not life itself an ongoing conversation?

The Lady

I didn't see her until I'd closed the door behind me, but she saw me. She paused from nibbling on my grass and looked warily over her shoulder as I emerged from the house.

I understood our conversation immediately. I kept my eyes down, only glancing up briefly. She seemed to understand my gesture. She kept her lovely eyes on me but flew no flag, watching as I walked to my car (which meant that I actually walked toward her) but still without focusing on her. It was satisfactory to her. I put forth no threatening signals.

In great silence and calm she watched me approach and open the door to my car. She was still chewing a bit of my lawn as she watched what I was doing with apparent interest.

I closed the car door as quietly as I could, then turned my back on her and retreated to the house again careful not to look directly at her. Once inside, I closed the door and only then did I look through the sidelight at her. She tossed her head formally and returned to her browsing.

Sometimes, there are meetings like this where nothing is said but all is understood.

Lost in a Hospital

The closest I could come to describing the experience of living with vascular dementia presented itself in a phone call from an old acquaintance. We were returning from our anniversary trip to Lexington. My acquaintance said he had had a heart attack and had been released by Kings Daughters but that he was still having chest pain and wanted us to drive him to Cabell-Huntington. We couldn't, of course, but as soon as we got home, I called him back. By then, he was in Cabell-Huntington's ER. He begged me to come talk to him, and I headed to Huntington.

Cabell-Huntington is constructed on the plan of an anthill – that is, there is no discernible plan at all to the layout of parking lots and doors. After many wrong turns, I found a large sign marked "Emergency" with a prominent arrow pointing right. I parked and started walking that way only to run into construction and a fence. I saw a door at the foot of some steps and went in. The door led to a corridor. That corridor led to another, and that to another. By then, I had no idea where I was in relation to the emergency room. I found someone to ask and eventually, many doors and corridors later, arrived at the ER.

After my time with my friend, I tried to retrace my steps. This is the point at which being lost in a hospital begins to mirror life with vascular dementia. All the corridors look the same. A few Exit signs led me to doors marked, "Emergency staff only" or "Do not open or siren will sound". In no time, I was hopelessly lost. Worse than that, I was disoriented. The experience mirrored a recurring nightmare I have in which I am on a familiar road which then becomes stranger and stranger. The longer I drive, the more lost I become. The corridors of Cabell-Huntington were replaying my nightmare exactly.

This is familiar to anyone who has ever gotten lost in a "modern" hospital, but I must view all such events through the lens of my diagnosis. Am I just lost as intended by the demonic architects who planned this nightmare, or have I had another clot, killing yet more of my brain? The more I walked, the more lost I became and the more the tears welled up, threatening to streak down my cheeks.

Somehow, I got outside. The only strategy I could imagine was to circle the hospital and hope to spot my little car. I started up the Emergency ramp. Not even half-way up my knees and my back began to remind me that a 75 year old man has no business asking them to do such a thing. Finally, the pain was so great that I sat on a guard rail, breathing heavily, head down. That's when I saw a security guard headed my way, masked, armed and wearing a bullet proof vest.

The young man asked if I was alright and I answered truthfully that I was not. One part of my mind seemed to still be functioning and what it perceived was an elderly dementia patient, obviously confused and in distress. That was my awakening, for that is just what I was. I held back the tears of fear and frustration with difficulty as I explained to the young man that I couldn't find my car.

The young man helped me back to the ER and got a wheelchair for me. When I was seated, he asked me questions about where my car might be, where I had entered the hospital, any landmarks I might recall. I couldn't answer any. My memory was gone. How had I entered the hospital? I did not know.

What happened next still takes my breath away. The officer began to push my wheelchair out of the ER and embarked on a tour of all the parking lots in the full heat of August. He even engaged another officer to help locate my little Nissan! He wheeled my dead weight around until we found my car. Well, that's to say HE found my car. I didn't recognize it at first.

If my experience in the wheelchair represents my life as this disease progresses, I am frightened, but the actions of this young officer in the deadly heat of August strengthens me. In these frankly awful times, it is still possible for one person to reach out to another, even at cost to himself, to ease suffering and offer comfort.

And so, as I rose to get in my car, the young man asked my name. He smiled and removed his mask. "Did you attend First Christian Church in Ashland?", he asked.

My jaw dropped open. The kind man was a childhood church friend of our daughter. It is a small world we inhabit, is it not?

Living Outside The Monkey Bars

The playground at Oakview Grade School featured two ranks of swings, two of teeter-totters and one monkey bar. This last was a marvel of iron pipe, roughly hexagonal in shape, each bar separated from the one above it by exactly the same distance, and all closed by a cupola supported by curved bars. Within the monkey bars, a child lived in a world of regularity. Climbing on the monkey bars was as predictable as the fall of the rain, each bar precisely where it was supposed to be, predictable and secure. I cannot adequately express the confidence generated by this venerable piece of playground equipment.

My disease has brought into awareness something I had not noticed before. We live within a web of connected memories and concepts, as interlinked as were the bars of the monkey bars. To think of Saturdays at the Capitol Theater brings to mind not only memories of the Capitol, but thoughts of my grandfather, or Saturdays during grade school with a day ahead of me filled with no obligations. I simply could not catalog the extent of this interconnected web for each such memory is also connected with its communicating notions, like an infinite monkey bar, secure in its predictability.

With dementia, those connections are broken and the web falls to pieces like a spider's web in a windstorm. At a breeze I am swept from the comfort of the center of the monkey bars to an exposed place where I am alone. It is horrible. It is frightening.

Those to whom I have shared this have offered me compassion and I am so grateful for that caring, but that doesn't reduce the certainty that these spells are but foretastes of my life going forward. It makes me morose, and I ask your forgiveness. I'm not seeking a pity party; I am only explaining how very challenging this new reality is to me. It will take some adjustment.

Treasuring Dead Ends

Mentally, we live within a web of connected memories and sensations. Memories are the ballast beneath my keel, but I'm losing my ballast because of multiple "infarcts". Any portion of my brain which has died for lack of oxygen is called an "infarct". The multiple infarcts in my brain mean that if a memory I seek should lie on the far side of such a roadblock, it is inaccessible unless a way can be found around it. The infarct marks a "dead end". Sometimes, my brain can find an alternative route; other times, not.

My busy brain frequently hits one of these road closed signs. You'd be surprised at how often. It makes me woozy. Perhaps that's why I find myself drawn, during my travels, to those roads which warn, "No Outlet" or "Dead End". I feel a sense of kinship with them. Like me, the dead ends grew organically, without a plan for a future. They served the needs which had called them forth, then, their purpose completed, settled into a slow decline as their resources dwindled, just as now do I. They arose to fit a present need, not as access to a future. Father came home from the war. It was time to begin a family. My parents did not set out to construct a lawyer or a pastor for the future. They set out to build a family for today. That was goal enough!

Time passed. The stories told along the dead end streets, stories of families, perhaps tragedies, births, deaths, successes, become ever more inaccessible to those in the present who see only dilapidated houses with overgrown lawns.

It is no wonder, then, that a dilapidated house or overgrown garden raises an aching sense of kinship within me. We did good work, the dead ends and I. We raised families. We stood against bad weather. We housed love. That those memories are now inaccessible does in no way reduce their worth.

The Old Stage Road

A few days ago, as my little granddaughter passed the flowers beside the porch, she was saluted by a beautiful Monarch butterfly, right in her face. After she admired him, she pointed at the flowers and commanded, "Now, go pollinate". That memory got the wheels in my aged head moving, considering the powerfully potent part purpose plays in all life, butterflies to humans. That thought, in turn, moved me to begin thinking on what damage a purposeless life might do.

I've written books before and they sold so many copies that I had to borrow money for lunch. Indeed, rather than books, they might be better characterized as exercises in creative typing. They were vanity projects. That is not to say they were purposeless. Their purpose was to bolster my vanity, and upon printing they did so. Thereafter, their purpose fulfilled, they sat idle, rather like I am doing now.

I've attached a photo of the "Old Stage Road" in Pollard. You'll notice that it is a dead end. At one time, there was a need for an acceptably smooth road upon which the stage could ride, and the Old Stage Road presumably answered that need. It had a purpose. It no longer has a purpose and now sits idle and dead ended. It is of interest only as a landmark out of its time.

True, I do have an obligation to my congregation and it takes me about three days to produce an acceptable sermon, but that is not three full days. The frailties of the flesh will allow me to work steadily no more than an hour or two a day before the energy is spent, so most of my day is as purposeless as is the Old Stage Road and I devolve into the old man's refuge of shouting at "those young kids" and wallowing in self-pity.

Beware, oh mortals, of a purposeless life!

Trapped on Lookout Street

The world attempts to educate me on my new status. Like a third grader, I resist until the lessons become strong enough to break through my resistance. Today, I was in line at Wendy's behind an absurdly jacked-up truck with enormous tires, a trumpet-like extension on his tailpipe to make the exhaust even louder, and a "Biden sucks" sticker in the window. This constellation normally speaks to me of ignorance, a child's mind in an adult body seeking respect and acceptance by a world unwilling to undertake the task on such terms as he offers. I normally answer such displays with contempt, but this time, I couldn't quite generate the emotion. I found that odd as I usually revel in contempt of others.

On my way home, sometimes I wander. I turned on to Simpson Road and went up Debord Hill just to see what is up there. What is there is appalling housing and roads that dead end. To live there, one must accept the appalling housing for there is no road away. One is trapped on Lookout Street. I thought about the driver of the truck. Now, instead of contempt, I felt kinship with him. He seemed to me to be trapped as well by his poor abilities and lack of skills, cast out of employment by a world which no longer had any call for his skill set. Then I felt contempt for myself. What business had I standing in judgment of him? I don't know him. I put the whole business out of my mind.

At home, I collected my mail. I had one official-looking envelope which said "Second notice". That always gets my notice. The envelope instructed me to tear off the tabs on each end then insert a finger and tear along the fold. I tried. I have a tremor. I could tear off the tabs, but separating the fold defeated me for the longest time. When I finally got it opened, it was an insurance offer and I became angry. The world had played upon my reaction to "second notice" to further frustrate me. The other mail was from my health insurance. It was a booklet of some tens of pages. I knew what I would find were I to attempt to read it – incomprehensible gobbledygook which would frustrate me even more by showing me how little it takes to defeat one such as I.

That's when the driver of the truck re-entered the conversation. Was this packet of mail like his world – important things that he had not the ability to understand, important actions he must take to remain a contributing part of his world but which the mere thought of undertaking defeated him? True, I still had no business putting myself in judgment of him. I don't know him, but I knew that there were many like I had imagined him to be – people trapped on Lookout Street in appalling housing for want of a marketable skill, or elderly people like me with no path forward.

Oh world! Why must your lessons be so painful? Is it to ensure that I pay attention?

My Ashland

ENTRANCE TO CLYFFESIDE PARK, ASHLAND, KY.

Like all mammals, humans evolved to live within a community which is defined by the community's culture. Meeting someone who shares culture with us is a signal of safety; meeting someone from a different culture is a signal for some degree of anxiety. Countless generations of evolution have baked that in to the bread.

Losing access to one's memories means losing access to one's culture. That explains why I ache so for My Ashland, the Ashland in which I was formed. I don't ache for it out of some sanitized nostalgia, for in many ways it was a dreadful place. Avondale was home to many, but it was not a nice place to live. Windsor Court was a nice place to live, but in its back was an open sewer and the nice people who lived there gave no thought to exposing their sewerage to any who dared that stream. No, I ache for My Ashland for it is where, at the last analysis, I belong and I know that it is drifting away from me. It was mother to me, raw sewerage, polluted air, racial divide and all.

My hunger for My Ashland leads me to streets never explored in my youth. I find myself drawn to such streets, convinced that a curtain exists somewhere upon them through which I might, at least, catch a glimpse again of My Ashland. When I follow these roads less traveled, what I find are abandoned homes, discarded dreams and calamities as great as are my memories of My Ashland fragile. Perhaps I'm trying to recall how my mind worked before the time when so many roads were closed.

Of course, modern man that I am, I could simply call up a map on my phone and be told exactly where each road goes, where it intersects, where it would take me, but that's not really knowledge, is it? It is mere data, and to imagine that accessing the mere data of our world is the same as having knowledge of it is foolishness.

All roads are significant. It is only our choices which make some seem trivial and so, I wander. Indeed, I wander so much that my wife has forbidden me from leaving the county for fear I shall find myself in unfamiliar territory be unable to find my way home again.

I understand that many older men do this. We are trying to recover that which time has taken, just as my mind scrambles its resources to find a way around a closed path to a sought memory. We look for summer days on bicycle wheels. We look for Boy Scout hill, covered with snow which flew past us as we hazarded the curves. Where did it go? Where are Mrs. Barber and the Oakview cafeteria? Where did Suzy go once the Parson's elevator was automated, making her redundant and her announcement of "Fifth Floor, toys" only a lovely memory?

The intersection of Belmont and 29th Street was known as "Geiger's Crossing". Who remembers that now, or Smitty's restaurant, he of the beef barbecue sandwiches and the ponies out back? Two of my neighbors, Mrs. Sheets and Mrs. Hodges, kept horses in my neighborhood. Is that memory only within me? Or the show ring on Grandview. Does anyone now recall the horse shows? All these things, once reliable bulwarks of stability, now gone, leaving only repurposed shells behind, dead ends whose purposes are now exhausted. I wander to return to them as living places that I might reconnect to my culture stolen from me by age and disease. That this cannot be done is evident, but I'm an old lion and old lions long to walk on familiar ground. We trust the past because it was the past which nurtured us. It is our home and community and we're lost outside of our community.

Today, to my enormous surprise, the past reached out to me. Not my past, but rather a past known only second hand even by my parents' generation. Clyffeside Park reached out to me.

While driving, my attention was drawn to a little creek which crosses beneath the road. I have crossed that creek countless times in my life but never paid it any attention. Now, it demanded a glance. When I could safely do so, I pulled over and checked a map. To my astonishment, the unprepossessing creek, scarcely a stride wide, was nothing less than Clyffeside Branch!

Clyffeside was before my time but its fame echoed through my childhood. As told by Jim Casto,

> ...beginning in the 1890s Ashland people began gathering at Savage Pond, fed by this same Clyffeside Branch. Children played ball and families picnicked. In the winter, there was ice skating on the frozen pond. The little park really took off in 1900 when the 50-acre property was purchased by the Ohio Valley Electric Railway. The trolley line named its new park Clyffeside and it quickly became the place to be and be seen. The park's centerpiece was a lake more than 350 feet wide and 1,500 feet long fed

by Clyffeside Branch. As time went by more and more attractions were added including a wooden roller coaster, a carousel, and a 3,000-seat "casino" (not for gambling, you understand, but for holding dances and shows). Even grander, the whole park was lit by electric lights! Ashland's first swimming pool was at Clyffeside. And, believe it or not, some of Marshall College's earliest football games were played there.

It would be hard to overstate the impact Clyffeside had on the community, particularly in view of its short span of existence.

And that was then. In the here and now, I'm pulled over in my car trying to reconcile the storied glamour of Clyffeside, its casino filled with mustachioed gentlemen and ladies in large hats, with the nasty, reed-choked little trickle below me. The grand past which reached out to me was a skeletal, decayed creek. There must be some mistake, I thought. I began to follow Clyffeside Branch for some trace of the glamour which I was convinced must remain. I arrived eventually at the water plant. Behind it is a Little League field and parking lots. Beside that is a muddy pond, all that remains of the storied lake of Clyffeside. No roller coaster. No carousel. No ladies in large hats. Just a city worker in a traffic vest collecting garbage.

Finally, I understood. I had been shown that the past is firmly passed. If it were somehow possible for the past to reach out to me, what I could perceive would be exactly what Clyffeside Branch showed me – a decayed and dirty disappointment, nothing more than a mute skeleton. Ashland and the people in it spoke to me in their time and that is enough. The past has little to say to me of the world in which I live for it is not its time.

The soil from which we spring always calls to us and that has not ceased. I am better prepared, though, for the disappointment which is all my wanderings will yield. Perhaps that is enough as well.

Peacock #8

I was born in 1946, a child of the horror known as the Second World War. The Second World War was the very essence of evil. How could an entire planet be at war? Oh surely, as the winners of the thing (whatever that might mean) we felt victorious, but somewhere in the decency we hide so well from ourselves was the certainty that we had killed, and not just armed soldiers. We won the war at the cost of so many lives, both theirs and ours that we had now to show that we were worthy of the victory. To celebrate our victory and to further distract ourselves from the awfulness we had done, we took to determined shows of propriety. To we children of the horror who bore none of the guilt, those shows of propriety were stifling.

As a child, I grew up on a street of well-maintained homes with neat lawns. It was not a spectacular neighborhood. It was thoroughly middle class, with the exception of a mansion owned by a one-time scrap dealer who began his career by pushing a hand cart, gathering up cans and trash from the streets, but finally made his fortune during the Second World War providing scrap for the war effort. His gracious home boasted a swimming pool and since the country club, that refuge of the well-to-do, did not permit membership to those of his faith, his swimming pool became the Jewish country club.

The street itself, surprisingly, was of brick, laid down by men with no hope of living on so gracious a street, in such well-maintained homes, but grateful for work which fit their hands. They labored, generations before my time, to fit brick after brick into beds of foundry sand, click! click! click! until brick pavement stretched like a red river. It was a comfortable place to grow up but a confining one. It was a secure furrow to nourish young minds in the well-ordered ways of the world but not a place to nourish imagination or a taste for mystery.

Behind the well-ordered houses, paralleling the fine brick paved boulevard was a single lane road, scarcely more than two dirt ruts, called Peacock #8. We called it "the alley" but we did so with an awareness of its alien nature. It did not belong to the well-ordered houses and the paved boulevard. It was of a different time.

Before the well-ordered houses were built, before the scrap dealer made his fortune, even before the men with the bricks, there was Peacock #8. It was built by the Peacock mining company to move coal extracted from the narrow seams of the hillsides. This was not coal mining in the modern sense. This was "stoop coal" – seams so low that only very small miners could dig it from its bed, and so it was – children with candles affixed to their caps, digging the coal from seams as low as three feet. Children shoveling the coal into mine buckets pushed by larger children down tracks only dimly still visible when I was a child to wagons pulled by mules which then traversed Peacock #8. Peacock #8 led from our neighborhood to a world that no longer existed, a world different from everything well-ordered and tidy along the brick streets that paralleled it. It was Peacock #8 that we boys followed to escape from the suffocating restraints of propriety. Peacock #8 was where we sated our taste for magic and mystery.

As the dirt ruts of Peacock #8 followed the hollow deeper into the woods, we boys could imagine that we were traveling far from the regularity of the brick streets, though, in truth, the woods we filled with such exciting mystery were only a short distance away from the boulevard. For us, though, that distance bordered on the infinite, for along Peacock #8 there were no regular brick laid streets and manicured lawns. There were no constrictions to a young boy's imagination. Down Peacock #8 lay the mystery for which we hungered with a hunger we would have been at a loss to explain to the adults in the well-maintained houses.

At last, Peacock #8 came to a bridge of thick wood. Not a romantic wooden bridge. A rough-cut, single lane affair over the tiny creek that followed Peacock #8 wherever it went. The bridge was as far as we were permitted to go, for beyond the bridge lay people, the descendants of the child miners perhaps, who were mistrusted by our parents and persons of considerable fear to us as their timid children attended school with us. People who raised such frightened children were not to be lightly engaged. There was rumor that they made whiskey somewhere below the bridge and that it would be death to uncover their still. Indeed, the belief was so strong that Wheeler's Grocery bore a sign warning that anyone buying more than 50 pounds of sugar must sign their book.

To the left of Peacock #8, though, was a path leading upwards along the hillside. As it was not, technically, beyond the bridge, we felt justified in following it, and follow it we did, to the mouth of a shelf mine. The layers of ancient sea bottoms had lifted and exposed a seam of coal perhaps three feet thick. We viewed it as a place of ineffable mystery, a tunnel into the very heart of the mountain, although in truth it was no more than 20 or so feet deep, the silt and the roof falls having closed whatever wound had been inflicted upon the hillside generations before we found it. We treasured and loved it and fancied all manner of trolls and other-worldly beasts living within it.

What was there about the mines that drew us to them down Peacock #8? The frightening area below the bridge is where my house now stands. There are no stills. There are no mountain trolls. There is now only an asphalt road intersecting the dim remains of Peacock #8. I walked it once. To travel from my house to my childhood home now would require that I walk over a well-mowed suburban lawn. The bridge has fallen to pieces. Peacock #8 in all its mystery lives only in my memory now. Do I live now in a world devoid of mystery, except in my mind? I would mourn a world without trolls, even now.

Father Hydrogen

I'm told by those who study these things that some 14+ billion years ago, there was a big bang. The joke among astrophysicists is that nobody knows what banged or what caused it to bang, but having done so, it began our universe. Before the bang, there is nothing – no space, no time, no place to stand to watch events unfolding until the event occurs, and that which was not becomes a hell of radiation. Those of a religious bent will find much familiar in this tale.

> In the beginning when God created the heavens and the earth, the earth was a formless void and darkness covered the face of the deep, while a wind from God swept over the face of the waters. Then God said, "Let there be light"; and there was light. [1]

So it was, say the astrophysicists. There was light, light of all kinds, radiation of all frequencies. They further tell me that in about 380,000 years (a meaningless unit of time, of course, because there is, as yet, no sun, no earth and therefore no year) things settled down enough for the first atoms to come into existence. Those atoms were of hydrogen – one proton, one electron.

At a later date, Mrs. Schneider's skillet arrived. Her skillet is of iron, and iron, in the astrophysical world, is poison to stars. Stars begin by fusing hydrogen into helium, releasing great quantities of energy. That energy counters the force of gravity which seeks to crush the mass of the star, and gives the star its life, a life which is a tug-of-war between the massive release of energy from the fusion of hydrogen into helium and the crushing force of gravity.

As things go along, the hydrogen is used up and the star begins fusing helium into other elements, releasing much less energy.

---

[1] Genesis 1:1-3 NRSV

This continues until, at last, the star produces iron. That is the end of the rope. The star explodes as a super-nova, ending the life of the star and scattering its core to eternity.

Those primordial hydrogen atoms and the iron are still here – the first fruits of the big bang and the remains of a star. The hydrogen is everywhere about us, even within us. Water is two atoms of hydrogen and one of oxygen. Oxygen is a much younger child of Creation, but Father hydrogen has been there virtually from the first. When you sip of the earth's good water, be aware that you are sipping of the first pressing of creation. And when you fry your eggs in the morning, be aware that you do so in the skeletal remains of a star beyond your imaginings. You drink from creation, and exist within eternity. It is worthy of gratitude.

Walking the Horseshoes

When I was young, my dad would occasionally propose a "hike" to me and my little brother. On one Sunday, he suggested, "Let's go walk the horseshoes".

"The horseshoes?", I asked.

"It's old Route 60", Dad responded. "It'll be fun". So off we went, past the city limits. Dad pulled off and led us to a small rise in the forest. To my great surprise, I stepped onto a brick street closely following the lay of the hill and forming, sure enough, a horseshoe around the small hollow. It was breathtaking to behold the geometric precision with which each brick had been placed, who knows how many years ago. All hand work, following the crooked old path the Cherokee made, for what Dad called "Old Route 60" was, in actuality, the transcontinental Midland Trail, established by General Washington in 1790 but in reality much older than that. It was ancient even to the Cherokee and the Shawnee, for it was known to the Adena as long ago as 800 B.C.E.

Years later, I attempted to revisit it. My goal in entering Armco Park was to walk it once again with the memory of that hike with my dad. That turned out not to be in the cards for 74 year old me. I did find the trail and tried to follow it down to the bricks. Old man knees complained, and, as happens more often than I would like to confess, my bladder demanded attention half-way down. I have learned that these alarms are to be ignored only at great peril to my wardrobe and since I was quite alone, I did what was needed. Honestly, I felt ashamed but then, a voice crossed my consciousness saying with contempt, "Do you imagine you are the first to have emptied your bladder here?"

In my mind's eye, Shawnee and Cherokee walked the trail again, contemptuous of the bricks. The Adena, as well, with their stone tools hunted along the trail. Life, all of life, flowed along the trail and I was now, in some way, part of a 3,000 year old transit of people walking the horseshoes. I was humbled beyond my ability to express it.

Bare Hills

It's winter and the leaves have fallen leaving the hills bare. I don't like this season. It robs me of the mystery I crave. When I was young, we boys did not follow Peacock #8 in the winter for in the winter the bare limbs of the trees, stripped of their concealing leaves, revealed how shockingly close our mysterious alley was to the suburban back yards on both sides. We sought escape. We sought trolls and reminders of the child miners of long ago, deadly moonshiners and adventure. Now, with the leaves fallen, I can see again the hills as they are – piles of dirt and rock. The Adena do not walk the horseshoes as they might have done under the cover of the forest. The Shawnee make no camps. There are no trolls, only piles of dirt and rock and I am verklempt in a world stripped of mystery.

No people can exist without an informing myth – an understanding of the deeper meaning of their existence. That of 21st Century America is materialism, which holds matter to be the fundamental substance in nature, and demanding that all things are the results of material interactions. In this view, the busyness in our minds, our creativity and even consciousness are mere by-products of material processes outside of which they cannot exist. It is as sterile as the bare hillsides, the very sterility which drove us boys into the woods of Peacock #8. There is no spiritual air to be found in the bare hillsides of materialism, nor even any language with which to discuss our loss, leaving us to suffer mutely.

It was not always so. The Adena could not have built their serpent mounds from such a sterile informing myth. The Shawnee and the Cherokee could not have built villages which sustained them in harmony with their world from such a foundation. It is our insistence on viewing our world as a mechanism understandable to our limited minds which has led us to strip the hills bare and to be satisfied by what we have created. It will not end well. No it won't, but to see that we need the language and wisdom our informing myth has banned us from even considering. We are, again, too soon smart and too late wise.

I found a path to salvation from this sterility in 8th Grade math and the Greek letter π. You may remember from Middle School that if you know the diameter, D, of a circle, you can find the circle's circumference, C, by multiplying the Diameter by the value of π, or C=πD. Doing a little algebra, we get the value of π=C/D, just as we said. OK. Exhale. No more math.

I still remember first learning that all I needed was a circle's diameter to instantly know its circumference and thinking what a totally cool thing that is. Except...the value of π can never be known exactly. It is an "irrational number". Measure the circumference of a circle, large or small, to within the width of an atom, measure its diameter to the same degree of certainty, get the biggest, fastest computer you can and divide the one by the other. It will never come out even. There will always be a remainder.

π is a fundamental constant, underlying all of mathematics, physics, architecture, you name it. Without π we wouldn't be able to chart the orbits of the planets. Our bridges would fall down. π is as real, as concrete as...well...as concrete. There is nothing hippy-dippy about π, no spiritual mambo-jumbo. It is as real as shoelaces, except...we can never know its value precisely. It is an irrational number governing a world we insist must be rational. No matter how carefully we measure and calculate, there is always a remainder and that remainder represents the unreachable soul of our world, that which is forever beyond us. It is where the trolls live.

We have been taught that there is no unreachable soul of our world, that all questions have answers, that nothing is beyond us. That this is not so is plain from π, but if you want to be excluded from further conversations, suggest that.

"Well, we can calculate π to whatever degree of accuracy we need, so it doesn't matter anyway and what in the world is wrong with you?"

There's still a remainder.

"I just don't care! That doesn't bother me a bit!"

There's still a remainder.

"Believe me, I've got a lot more important matters on my calendar than that!"

There's still a remainder.

We have left behind the humanizing quality of humility in our arrogant pursuit of rationality. Perhaps it is time to acknowledge our need for the occasional troll.

Intersecting Contributions

As I sink into my "twilight years" and my vision dims, I find I am drawn to certain places from my younger years.

I am drawn to the site of my maternal grandfather's house and its three grand walnut trees, older, I fancy, than the Cherokee. I am drawn to Peacock #8.

Clyffeside Branch taught me that these visits are no mere nostalgic visits to my past. They are, rather, exhumations. In place of my grandfather's house, I find a modern home and the remains of one of Granddad's honored walnut trees cruelly hacked down. Peacock #8 is lined with garbage cans and dead ends into a driveway leading to a grand home, the fabled bridge now gone to dust and decay.

Strangely, I am not drawn back to other places in my past. My paternal grandfather's home is unchanged from my childhood, the years having left no more trace of their passing than did he during his occupancy. Granddad did not like change. I wander in pursuit of a past long departed, not one now disturbingly present.

I suspect that my wiser friends would counsel me to let go of the memories of a dead past and to focus my attention on the time given me now. I suspect such advice will go unheeded for I wish to live fully, with consciousness of both present experience and my memories of the past. Life is ever-changing. I have no desire to live like my grandfather's house, as a static monument.

My two grandfathers gave me two very different views of life. My maternal grandfather didn't think about life. He just did. He wound up a poor man. My paternal grandfather was a stern man who would suffer no crying after spilt milk. If your choices led to bad consequences, you learned from those consequences and did not repeat the error, but neither did you weep over this opportunity to learn, however painful those consequences might be. He wound up a wealthy man and I am still living on some of his money, having wisely chosen to outlive the rest of my family. One grandfather contributed much to his community but little to me as a person; one contributed little to his community, but much to my childhood and developing world view. One had little to contribute to my youth, but I'm still benefiting from his wealth. The other left me nothing but a handmade toy canon, but his absence from my childhood would have made a tragic difference in my life.

The Beast Stalks

Each of us, I believe, is given a role in the family. That role defines, at least in part, the self-image with which one lives thereafter. If it is a good self-image, all is well; if it is toxic, then much of subsequent life must be devoted to discrediting it and finding a more positive self-image.

In my family, my assigned role was "the smart one". My brother, Jimmy, was "the one who struggles". He wound up as "The Flying Dutchman" on WKEE and was beloved by his listeners. I wound up as a morose ex-lawyer which should tell you something of the accuracy of my thoughts on this topic, but we'll move on.

My family role as "the smart one" meant that any deviation from excellence struck at the very foundations of who I was. If I got a B-, that meant I wasn't as smart as I was supposed to be, and thus, wasn't really me. That's an unkind thing to saddle a child with. It made me fragile. Nonetheless, I did have mental resources and I continued with good grades. Over my shoulder, though, stalked the beast, "The Smart One", always waiting to pounce and cast me out of the family role assigned to me.

That beast still stalks me and revels in my loss of abilities through the progress of my dementia. Recently, dementia took from me the ability to balance my checkbook, a task I had assigned to myself decades ago. Weekly I assured that there was money to pay the bills and as "The Smart One" I took great pride in it. Now, the computer, rather than the compliant servant it has always been, has become a stranger and the beast howls in victory. If I am no longer the Smart One, I am no longer me! I feel a great need for someone to throw me a rope as a friend did in high school.

In school, as it became more challenging to always excel in the classes offered, I adopted a strategy of embracing activities others didn't so I could claim, by even mediocre facility, to still be "the smart one". I chose chess. That meant I needed a partner. A school friend filled the bill and more so. He was much the superior player. To this day, I cannot recall ever besting him. He played by intuition and played very well. You would think that such an experience would have played right into my insecurities and driven me from chess and my opponent, but it did not. To this day, I think back on that time and wonder at the way he handled so poor an opponent as was I.

He did it by winning games without ever beating me. He won the games, but his success never translated into victory over me. He held me in high regard and somehow made me understand that victory on the board did not involve in any way a lessening of me, a message radically different from that offered by the stalking beast! To this day, when things conspire to defeat me, my mind goes back to that chessboard and I come to see each failure of my day as something other than defeat. His kindness granted to me a lifetime of resiliency.

We remained friends through adulthood and well into old age. He continued to offer me that same strength against adversity which he had offered over the chessboard and I continued to lap it up. Then, one day he drove me to a music festival (my doctor had taken my car keys due to this damnable disease). We were out of state, so we felt we could get away with sharing the driving. As we climbed the hill to the festival, I was idly thinking of the many contributions he had made to my life over the years and said, in jest, that I wished I wasn't so dependent upon his approval.

I meant no great confession. It was just something that came into my head, but my friend reacted with a roar! "Oh! Don't say that! How do we go on from here now?" He was in a froth over an observation I thought both of us were aware of. He was in real distress at the thought, and I was felled by guilt. His kindness while thumping me over the chessboard, while supporting me over the bumps of life, while offering encouragement for my little projects had come from him completely unconsciously. He thought we were friends with common interests. My thoughtless words revealed that I viewed his many kindnesses as a substitute for that which I did not receive from my own family and he hated such a notion.

Thereafter, our friendship cooled. I can understand why, though I am still so very saddened by the experience. Life is dynamic and friendships are a part of life, perhaps its essence.

> **"The Moving Finger writes; and, having writ,**
> **Moves on: nor all thy Piety nor Wit**
> **Shall lure it back to cancel half a Line,**
> **Nor all thy Tears wash out a Word of it."1**

Be conscious, child. Not all that seems truth to you is the truth, the full truth, nor yet, nothing but the truth.

The Capitol Theater

I grew up in a changing town, much of it past its shelf life. My guide into Ashland-as-it-was was my grandfather, Marvin Stewart. Granddad was born in 1885, and his father was rumored to have hosted Wild Bill Hickok in his saloon. Earlier in the century, Granddad was co-owner of Capitol Amusements which ran numerous theaters. By the time I knew him, Granddad's responsibility had been reduced to taking the evening's receipts from the Capitol Theater, one of those he once co-owned, to the bank each morning. I do not know what caused his precipitous fall. It appears that the decade between 1920 and 1930 dealt him a serious financial blow and when I knew him, he was in much reduced circumstances. I asked the grandson of his partner if he knew. He said not, but added, "I do know that we gave him some little job." That speaks of charity and charity is often born of pity. It must have been calamitous.

The Capitol was built in the early years of the 20th Century to serve as a Vaudeville venue and was only later converted to a movie theater. I remember it fondly, though it, like our town, was well past its prime when I knew it.

On Tuesdays, we kids got to go with Granddad and view the theater by the light of day. Entering the Capitol to see a show was one thing. Entering the Capitol on a Tuesday morning when it was dark, silent and empty was quite another. Inside the theater one turned right and climbed three steps to a landing. From there, one could again turn right and climb more steps to the surprisingly mundane theater office. In view of the adventures we watched at the Capitol, the quite ordinary office was a jarring sight. The office held no interest for me.

However, once the first three steps had been climbed, provided no audience was present, one might also turn left from the landing and go to the balcony. We children who asked to go to the balcony during a show were told that the balcony was not structurally sound but the real reason was that it was reserved for "the coloreds". That made the balcony simultaneously mysterious, dangerous and intriguing so it was no surprise that on one Tuesday I ventured to the balcony. It was breath-taking. In the center, against the back wall, was the projection room from which a cone of light pierced the dusty dark air during a show to appear on the screen as actual moving pictures. Had we troubled ourselves to do so, we could have seen the cone of light containing the heroes and villains as it emerged from the balcony, but the dusty cone of light was incomprehensible to us. We had come to witness for ourselves the victory of good over evil and we were not troubled to ponder how that came to be.

The seats of the balcony were arranged as on the floor below, simultaneously quite normal and yet unique because from the balcony my point of view was elevated and I looked down on the seats below. It was in the balcony that I reached across immeasurable time, back to the silent film days and before the silent films to Vaudeville. On the balcony railing, I found a button. What could it possibly do?

I can't begin to tell you the thoughts which flashed through my mind at finding this bit of Aladdin's treasure nestled under the balcony lip. Was it a fire alarm? Would it summon police? Prudence demanded that the button not be tampered with, but it called to me! Without the least conscious effort, my hand was drawn to the button, stroking it but not yet depressing it. I was frightened and compelled at the same time. I don't recall deciding to do so but my finger jabbed it. Immediately, the theater was filled with a hellish wail, easily the most enormous sound I could imagine. I wet my pants.

At first, I had no idea what I had unleashed, then at nearly the same instant, I recognized a Klaxon horn! Whether silent movie or Vaudeville sound effect I couldn't say, but in that instant my young life was connected with the vaudeville shows and silent movies more than half a century past. I was, at one time, there, in the present and also laughing with the crowds who had just been frightened out of their wits by the Klaxon horn in the dark.

The silent movies and the Vaudeville shows were long gone before I wandered the balcony of the Capitol Theater. The calamity which had reduced my grandfather from co-owner of a chain of theaters to his work when I knew him is also long gone and lost but not absent. Its shadows mark our present if we can chance upon the button.

The Saturday Club

Saturday was our parents' date night and my brother and I, along with our two cousins, were taken to the Capitol, arriving midway through the first feature and leaving midway through the second. Calling these films "features" is to grant them unwarranted status. The Capitol showed, for the most part, B Westerns.

Separating the two horse operas shown on Saturday night was "the Saturday Club". The first feature reached its conclusion with the good guy riding off into the sunset and the bad guy dead as befits all bad guys, though for us who had entered in the middle it was never clear why he was bad. The lights came up and Granddad climbed the steps, disappeared around the red velvet curtain, and returned with a wooden table painted silver upon which rested a large jar with the ticket stubs for the evening. Granddad stirred the stubs with a wooden spoon, then called on a child from the audience who mounted the stage and drew a ticket, entitling the holder to a cake from Grandview Dairy. The table and jar were returned, and we watched half of the second feature.

One Saturday, in perhaps 1954, and to my great surprise, I was picked to pull a ticket from the jar. Trembling, I climbed the steps and peeked around the curtain. To my astonishment, I found a world there, a remnant of the day long past when the Capitol hosted live shows. Stage left held a complicated arrangement of ropes, wires and cables against the possibility that the elderly curtains would ever again need to be drawn as they once had been for Vaudeville shows. More astounding yet, a separate system of ropes and pulleys, which perhaps once had lifted and lowered stage elements and backgrounds in vaudeville shows, now had been adapted to raise or lower the screen. I was dumbstruck. A screen? Which could be raised? We kids in the darkness of the Capitol theater never entertained the thought that we were watching images cast upon a screen, so intense was our concentration on the story unfolding before us. This is what we came for, the victory of the good guy over the bad guy and the vindication of good over evil. Yet, here, beyond argument, was a tattered screen hanging loosely before an ordinary brick wall, not the plains of Texas we had watched projected. In this instant I came to see how fragile are the illusions we watched so raptly on the screen and I wondered, "What other realities we take so seriously might also be illusions on a tattered screen?"

I think of the Saturday Club on my drives up Prospect Hill or other places connected in my mind with Granddad. I am still, a lifetime later, trying to come to terms with the reality behind the darkening, shortening illusion I live. The first feature each Saturday, which we saw only from the middle on, showed us the conclusion to a plot to which we were not party, just as the life I was dropped into had its beginnings long before I arrived. The second feature, of which we saw only half, developed a black plot, the resolution to which would be forever denied me.

Reflecting on these memories, I began to see how important were my experiences at the Capitol Theater to my world view today. It was in the Capitol that I first saw the ropes which supported what I had taken for reality, giving me my first hint that there might be something more within the cone of light that flickers above us than the reflection which we could see. Such a revelation has colored my certainties since that time.

Kyle Rittenhouse

Many of the B Westerns we watched, either side of the Saturday Club, featured Sunset Carson. Sunset, the very image of the good guy, was played by Michael Harrison, an Oklahoma rodeo star and a terribly flawed man who eventually self-destructed. So much for the bright division line between the good guys and the bad guys. Whatever demons preyed on Harrison, Sunset Carson was the clean-cut good guy, was he not? His clothes are laundered. His Colt is white-handled. Even more telling, his gun belt is loaded with a glut of cartridges, enough for an extended fight except… they appear to be crimped blanks and they extend around the belt, putting them behind him, were he wearing the gun belt. Like the screen in the Capitol Theater, one might well begin to suspect that all is not as it is being presented.

The pistol is an icon of American manliness – a Colt .45 single action. If ever there was a weapon which more precisely captures the image of American manliness, I don't know what it might be. This is the gun that won the west during the countless B westerns we sat through at the Capitol Theater. Replicas of this pistol were what we wanted for Christmas. But by 1940 these pistols were hopeless antiques. They are too slow to load, even without having to reach behind you for the cartridges. Army issue had been the 1911 Colt semiautomatic for 30 years by the time Sunset rode. This pearl-handled beauty is offering something other than utility to us, despite the abundance of cartridges displayed.

This country was formed on the hope that free individuals would willingly set aside their stubbornness in favor of a social contract arrived at by consensus of the majority. Sunset's gun belt shows us just how little traction this idea has enjoyed historically. The totem to which we bend the knee is the ideal of the individual, rather than any loyalty to the society which supports us. Young

Kyle Rittenhouse, who shot three people, killing two, in Kenosha, Wisconsin can misrepresent himself as an EMT and deputize himself to act outside of the contract agreed to by "We the people", even to commit homicide in the name of "I the person" and still secure the approval of a jury of twelve. This is the totem Sunset Carson displays – not an antique weapon, but the symbol of the unfettered individual, an individual who has freed himself by his supposed virtue from the constraints of the social contract which should define America. It is a symbol of the vigilante which lies at the heart of so many in America and is antithetical to our commitment to America as a community of individuals acting for the good of the whole.

One of the ladies on The View today asked when was the last time our country viewed itself as a unified land. One of the other ladies answered "The Eisenhower administration". I wouldn't argue the details but certainly if we don't, and soon, redefine ourselves as Americans living within a social contract in which we are each personally invested even if we disagree on the details, then we shall answer Lincoln's words at Gettysburg, "Now we are engaged in a great civil war, testing whether that nation, or any nation so conceived and so dedicated, can long endure" with even more tragedy.

Sunset Carson and the countless other like entertainments depicting the immunity of the good guy from any constraints planted this seed. We reap a whirlwind.

Jonathan Smithers

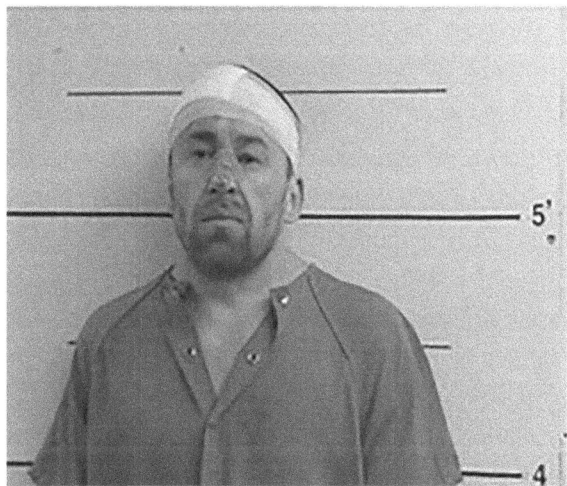

I have been shaken by this man. As reported by the Daily Independent,

"The suspect believed to be behind the Monday morning shooting of a Flatwoods Police Officer was wanted on a child pornography indictment out of Boyd County, according to court records.

Jonathan L. Smithers, 41, of Catlettsburg, was released less than two years ago after serving 17 years in jail for stabbing a 10-year-old girl during a home invasion in 2003. A mere 20 months after his release, Smithers would be accused of shooting officer Tommy Robinson in the neck."

I was the prosecutor who got him that 20-year sentence, while working closely with the girl and her mother. I still remember the morning after the attack. Kathy and I went to her hospital room as soon as we heard only to find the room filled with balloons and other gifts from law enforcement. This was a rotten attack on a helpless child and that sort of thing does not happen in our town. Everyone was revolted.

Taking the case to trial would have increased the child's trauma by forcing her to take the stand so we settled on the maximum 20 year sentence to save her that trauma. Kathy says we also resisted parole, and I recall sending letters. Kathy says we were unsuccessful but 17 years out of a 20-year sentence sounds like a serve-out to me. Anyway, in only 20 months of freedom he has been charged with child porn and with having shot a brave policeman. I pray for his swift recovery.

Apart from the revolting things he is accused of, why should this man shake me? I spent 30 years dealing with "criminals". What is different about him? I'm going to tell you.

When the man on the street thinks of a criminal, that word defines the man. He can accept that there are good cops but also some bad cops. He cannot entertain the possibility that there are "good criminals". Those of us in law enforcement, though, come across some from time to time. I'm thinking of a spectacularly unsuccessful car thief the cops dubbed "Shady Grady". Shady Grady compulsively stole cars. He wasn't particularly good at it and we always caught him. If memory serves, I asked him once why he kept stealing cars. He replied that he just loved cars.

Eventually, he stopped stealing cars and went straight! He even started a business. Doing what, you ask? Selling cars, of course.

One night there was a noise outside his house. He investigated and saw a man running from the convenience store with the cash register under his arm. Shady Grady tackled the man to the ground. When the police arrived, the man was screaming, "I didn't do nothin'! Let me up!"

Grady yelled back, just as loudly, "I'm a convicted felon! I know a robbery when I see one!"

Yes, children, it is possible to be a good criminal. This is why Walter Wink's words have governed my thoughts about good people and bad people for so many years:

If only it were all so simple! If only there were evil people somewhere insidiously committing evil deeds, and it were necessary only to separate them from the rest of us and destroy them. But the line dividing good and evil cuts through the heart of every human being. And who is willing to destroy a piece of his own heart?

However much you'd like to divide God's children into good guys and bad guys, we've all got some of both in us. That's been my understanding for decades. Then, along comes Jonathan Smithers. I don't know what to do with Jonathan Smithers. I can perceive nothing but evil in what he has done, and that's above my pay grade.

"Do not judge, so that you may not be judged. For with the judgment you make you will be judged, and the measure you give will be the measure you get. Why do you see the speck in your neighbor's eye, but do not notice the log in your own eye? Or how can you say to your neighbor, 'Let me take the speck out of your eye,' while the log is in your own eye? You hypocrite, first take the log out of your own eye, and then you will see clearly to take the speck out of your neighbor's eye."

I know Jesus' words from Matthew. I believe that I have not the wisdom to judge even Jonathan Smithers but I am shaken. Is there any good in the man? I do not see any, but I cannot see him. And the truth is I do not want to see him. My sin is palpable.

The Stranger in the Cemetery

One afternoon I found myself at the West Kirby Flats cemetery beside the grave of my great-great grandfather, Alvin Stewart. Alvin fought for the Union with Company C of the 14th Kentucky Infantry. When Alvin Stewart was born on a farm in Lawrence County, Kentucky, Abraham Lincoln was 15 years old. He couldn't know of me then, nor at the end of his life in 1907, ten years before my father was born. We are perfect strangers, yet his influence is still to be found somewhere in every cell of my body.

His grandson, Marvin, was my beloved Granddad Stewart, a man I loved more than I can say, but they really had no connection, either. I first encountered Alvin at the kitchen table at Granddad's house when I asked him about his family. After a searching pause, he told me that his grandfather was named Alvin but that he lived "very far away", he thought West Virginia, and he had never met him.

That conversation sparked an interest in genealogy, and I eventually found the divorce papers by which my great-great grandmother divorced him in absentia. The divorce papers contained an affidavit from his son, my great grandfather, saying that he had not seen his father since Christmas. Alvin was a successful and diligent farmer before the war. After the war, he abandoned his family. It was heart-breaking to read. Have I a villain in my DNA, or a 19th Century victim of PTSD?

Unlike the characters on the screen of the Capitol, he most probably was both as are all of us. Were we to somehow meet, would I think of him as honorable, or not? How would I measure honor in any event? I was confusing myself by chasing a tail with no dog attached.

"Hello, old grandfather!", I greeted him as I lowered myself next to his grave. In this well-maintained cemetery (by whom, I wonder?) there are fenced off sections which I presume represent family units. One, centered upon a large American flag on a tall pole contains a lot of Stewarts (some with impressive stones) along with other surnames but no Alvin. Alvin lies on the outside of the cable beneath a poor veteran's stone. His ex-wife, my great-great grandmother, is buried in pomp and circumstance in the Ashland Cemetery beneath a grand stone.

It was Memorial Day on which I first chose to visit and I brought a flag to place at his grave. The other veterans had flags, but none for Alvin. Instead, I found a tiny plastic flower planted approximately over where his heart must be. If a "villain", was he nevertheless still remembered with affection? I made a second visit and found that someone had dug up his hand-carved foot stone and re-erected it. Who would have done such a kindness for a forgotten old veteran?

"Well, old grandfather. What sort of fellow were you?", I asked. "Your grandson, Marvin, said you lived far away. Obviously, you did not." Were you a family embarrassment not to be discussed?

"Your grandson was a man of unsound judgment, but a loving and lovable old man nevertheless. Like you he was poor. His family suffered mightily during the depression and I think, because of that, your great granddaughter, my mother, became so emotionally distant that when she died my father tried to console me by telling me, 'I know she didn't always show it, but she really loved you boys.' Was that, instead, an echo of your DNA? Were you emotionally distant as well? Did you wind good or evil into the spirals of my DNA? Must I expect further mischief? What do you think, old grandfather?"

Alvin chose not to speak.

Alvin's contributions to my perspective are as incomprehensible as was the cone of light in the dusty air of the Capitol.

"Old grandfather, my generation is all but gone. I have one first cousin living, but he has children, and grandchildren. And his sister had children and perhaps grandchildren. I have one living child and two grandchildren, so your line still has life in it. What do you contribute? Are you just another stranger in the cemetery, or is there more of you in us than that? Do you still speak?"

As usual, he failed to comment, but I felt strangely better, as usual. Villain or not, his DNA is a part of me, and that is as it must be.

The Etna Mission

Kathy and I have begun eating our lunch, weather permitting, at the Port of Ashland, a location on the banks of the Ohio improved by the city to include statuary and places to loaf. Sitting there watching the Ohio flow by is a most satisfactory centering experience.

Across the river, on the Ohio side, is a bluff formed when the highway was built. The hill was sliced as neatly as by a cleaver to make room for Route 52 and the bridge approaches. The slice reveals millions of years of seafloor, layer upon compacted layer, lifted unknown time before to form this hill. The top of the hill drew my eye. I became curious what might be up there. It was an unbroken ridge of green, with no sign of a structure.

When I was a boy, Carlyle Tile quarried clay from the top of the adjoining hill, hauling this least ancient seafloor down in carts pulled by donkeys, then across a bridge to their plant. We kids looked sharp for the donkeys, but I don't think we ever saw them, though we heard of them often enough from our parents. On occasional Sundays, Dad took my brother and me there to climb the hill to the top and look back over the Ohio to our town.

But that was the next hill down river. The hill before me as we ate our lunch at Port of Ashland was one unvisited, as far as I can recall. The more I looked at the slightly rolling top, the more curious I became what I might find, were I still vigorous enough to make the climb. I took out my phone and looked up Google maps.

Up came a sea of green, for the satellite had passed over at the height of summer. There was the bluff, seen from miles above, there the river, there Route 52. And centered in all this indistinctness was a pin. Places in Google maps, not otherwise identified, are marked by a red pin. This pin in the indistinct sea of green, marked the location of "Etna Mission" – except there was no mission, no structure of any kind, to be seen. Someone, or some bizarre algorithm deep in the bowels of Google maps, insisted that this location was not to be consigned to history's myths along with the donkeys. This spot was proudly to be noted.

Dad and my little brother are gone now, along with the donkeys, and save for my memories, they are as anonymous as Etna Mission. Also gone, as I looked again, is the red pin. It, too, has gone the way of the Cherokee, as we all must. All honor to you, Etna Mission, whatever you may have been.

The Waters of our Birth

This is the view from Virginia point of the mingling of the waters of the Big Sandy as it enters the Ohio river. Two very different waters, from two very different sources, each carrying very different experiences flow together and then proceed as one, no longer separate but not altogether merged, either. Each carries with it the memory of their source.

We are, each of us, complex amalgams of ancestral DNA, personal experience and cultural heritage. We don't think about that last contribution often, but it is the waters of our birth and informs us through life even as we mix and mingle the waters of our birth with that of those we meet.

The waters of my birth taught me to honor the traditions of my people, even when those traditions – coal mining, steel making and oil refining – did harm to both the environment and the health of the people. I've been a cop and a prosecutor, a police dispatcher and a commercial radio host. I've been a student and a college instructor, a voracious reader and an author. I have designed computer software for which people paid good money. I've even been a politician, holding two terms as Commonwealth's Attorney for Kentucky's 32nd Judicial Circuit. I am now a "stated supply speaker", something less than a pastor, in a Presbyterian Church. I have done all these things, but I am none of them. Like every child of the Hanging Rock Iron Region, I am a steel maker. Steel making wets the hands of all who live here.

I have a friend who lives a continent away in Seattle, a place I think of as "the place where they do things correctly". High educational attainment, clean air and water, and rational, data-driven actions characterize the place. If you have never visited Seattle or Portland, I hope you can do so. It is beautiful. The people are friendly; the environment clean; the food spectacular.

My friend and I had conversed on the net for some time, but had not yet met in person when she announced that she could come for a visit. The stage was set for a mingling of the waters. The day finally came. At my door was my Internet friend, masked against the virus. That's when it occurred to me that my mask was in the car. Then I made it worse – without thinking, I opened my arms for a big hug! That's what we do in Appalachia when someone comes to visit. She took a few steps backward. I felt a perfect idiot.

Once we were properly masked and socially distanced, I invited her into our living room. She looked around uncertainly before sitting. Eventually, she told us that our laminate wood flooring had been found to out-gas dangerous substances. Once again, I felt a perfect idiot and suggested that we move to the outdoor porch where she might feel more comfortable.

It was chilly on the enclosed porch and I saw her eyes move to the electric heaters we had running. "We had those once", she said, "but they take so much electricity that we replaced them all with solar heaters to reduce the amount of coal which has to be burned." The waters of her birth honor the environment.

Mentally, I was trying to calculate what it would cost to "go solar" in our comfortable home, when I realized that we live up a holler where the sun don't shine. Even if we wanted to do that, our very geography forced us into being consumers of polluting coal!

The waters of our birth trickle through our hands, and leave their traces on our fingers, often scarcely noticed. That slight dampness in part defines each of us. I recall driving a Vietnamese client to court in rural Kentucky. There was road work underway, and a blast went off. My client dove for the floor, wailing, "Oh me! Bombs come!" Her hands had been wet by the waters of war. My hands were wet as well by my culture and that remaining dampness permits me to view as normal things which are unacceptable to those from different waters.

I remember being driven to school in the morning by my dad because the "fog" was so thick that it would have been hazardous to walk – I might not be seen by a passing car until it was too late. I also remember my father driving with his door open and his head stuck out because the "fog" coated the windshield. We didn't question that. How could "fog" be hazardous to our health? It could because it was not fog at all. It was the residue the blast furnaces and the refinery pumped out thoughtlessly for us to breathe as best we could. My friend later recounted that she was made ill by the air quality here even though by the time of her visit the morning "fogs" were barely a memory. I apologized for the harm we had done her, and tried to explain that life dampens each hand differently. Our hands had been wet by poor air and water, more sickness than we should have had, but it is home to us, nonetheless.

I knew that my friend's comments were correct. Bad air and bad water, extra sickness and all that goes with that are terrible prices to pay for a living. I agreed with my friend, and yet I was defensive. Steel making is the waters of my birth! I remember the day Bellefonte Furnace was melted down in Amanda Furnace. I remember my classmates whose families Bellefonte and Amanda fed. Yes, they extorted a terrible price, but they granted us our identity. My friend's accurate and well-placed comments were blows struck at the roots of our existence which we find in our traditions, the dampness of life upon our fingers.

We are, each of us, complex amalgams of ancestral DNA, personal experience and cultural heritage, the waters of our birth. The water that leaves Virginia Point does not flow on as an eternal competition between the waters of the Ohio and that of the Big Sandy but as an amalgam of the two. Life, hopefully, is filled with opportunities to mingle the waters of our birth with that of others, for such meetings force us to examine our own. What emerges is neither one nor the other, neither adoption nor abandonment but a new amalgam of expanded experience. Such a thing is to be celebrated.

The Engine Wiper

I've had two conversations this week about welfare recipients. That's actually two more than I average in a week, but they both sounded such common themes that I am compelled to set out my thoughts about social safety net programs so that I can understand the issues better, if for no other reason.

The first conversation was with a lady a bit older than myself who shared that she and her husband, "... resent been taxed to death in order to support people who have never done an honest day's work in their lives." The second was with a lady very much younger than I, a law student, who wanted to work for welfare reform because the current system pays people "... who don't want to do anything but sit on their butt all day".

Obviously, these two ladies have painted with a much too broad brush, gathering all welfare recipients into a single, resentment-worthy group of ne'er do wells whose defining characteristic is laziness, and have used this straw man as the focus for their resentment of taxation. Equally obviously, each would confess that there are some people receiving public assistance who are disabled. Both would estimate such people to be in the minority, I suspect. Furthermore, each believes that labor, sacrifice and commitment to a disciplined life grants ownership of resources, giving them a say in its distribution.

I suppose that is a pretty widely-held position and one self-evident to everyone, but I would suggest that the resources being conserved belonged first to God. I am fairly confident that God's wishes do not include hoarding of resources in the face of suffering, though I am willing to listen to rational argument to the contrary, if any there be. It's a glass half full, glass half-empty argument. I would concede that there are lazy people with phony disabilities, but I believe that there are more powerful forces at work than simple laziness.

Dr. King noted that it is a cruel jest to say to a bootless man that he should pull himself up by his bootstraps, and worse yet if someone is standing on the boot. This is my view of our current conundrum ... someone is standing on the boot. I come to this conclusion based on my limited observations of my own community. Here is what I observed: When I was a child, Armco Steele Company employed roughly 5,000 people. Semet-Solvay, which made coke for the blast furnaces employed perhaps another 750. Secondary education in Ashland's Schools offered two tracks: college prep and labor reserve. Those who clearly were not going to college applied for labor reserve when they graduated high school. From then on, virtually to the grave, they flopped sheets, or were cinder snappers or skull knockers at Armco. They lifted and toted. They cleaned the soot holes under the massive blast furnaces. It was tough, dirty and dangerous work, but it was good for a lifetime, and it paid a living wage.

Today, AK Steele employs perhaps 500 people, and Semet-Solvay is closed. Where do those 4,500 people who once had work apply for employment? How valuable are the skills of a laid-off cinder snapper? Where is the industry which will compensate a skillful soot hole cleaner sufficiently to permit him to pay his mortgage and support his family?

Our world, like Ashland, Kentucky, is moving from a heavy industry economy to an information economy. That is a treacherous, perilous passage. Sadly, it is not negotiable by all. I recently watched a special on the Union Pacific's steam program. (Yes, the UP still runs some steam locomotives.) They were firing up one of the Challengers for an excursion. It took 48 hours to get it running. The engine was cared for by firemen, and boilermen, engine wipers, mechanics, and inspectors. Those were the jobs that existed wherever steam locomotives went, in every town on the line. Those jobs no longer exist. Where do the engine wipers apply for employment that pays as well as the railroad paid?

The reality of our world is that the engine wipers and the skull knockers, the cinder snappers and the manual laborers that once existed in such plenty in our country now find that the only alternative to unemployment is in the fast food industry, and fast food paychecks will NOT pay the mortgage. One couple of my acquaintance have collectively worked for 40 years at the same pizza restaurant. They are paid 10¢ above minimum wage. Why? They can be replaced at any time from the ranks of the 9.5% unemployed should they quit. Could they not improve themselves by finding better jobs? No...both are mentally impaired. They are unemployable anywhere outside the repetitive fast food market. Which will pay them minimum wage no matter where they go.

I said that it was a glass half-empty, glass half-full argument and such it is. The ladies who were speaking to me fear enabling laziness more than they empathize misery. I worry about the woman with a master's degree in Social Work who rides an electric wheelchair aimlessly around town because her mind has flown. I worry about the engine wipers, and feel that the risk of enabling ne'er do wells can be handled administratively. I don't believe that the unemployment rate is at more than 9% because people are lazy. Instead, I think they are unemployed because the corporations which own this country value their lives less than they value the bottom line. I don't believe it is reasonable to blame the unemployed for their plight in light of the growing understanding that our economic woes aren't the result of welfare frauds, but of corporate greed, and a decision way up the line to stop creating wealth, and to begin consolidating wealth at the expense of the most vulnerable.

Today, I passed a Christmas display in front of a house. The owner had cut out and painted plywood carolers in Edwardian dress and placed them in front of his house. The were in good voice, each face up-tilted, each mouth caught mid-syllable. I thought of these plywood figures spending most of the year in the back of the garage, their eyes still uplifted in hope, their mouths still open in silent song, heard by none, ignored by all.

Rather like an unemployed engine wiper.

The Silent Voice

A friend wrote,

> "You know, I thought that in America we are free to make
> our own choices and that we need to respect each other
> even if we disagree. Well as much as I disdain the extreme
> right and their intolerance, I've realized that I also decry
> the tyranny of the left where if you don't go along with
> their view of things you are criticized and insulted by the
> PC Police."

I spun a tale in reply:

> I want to delve into what you have said a bit more
> deeply, particularly the invocation of the "PC Police".
> To do so, I'd like to clear away the confounding aspects
> of contemporary conflicts and reconstruct a reasoned
> conversation occurring about 1860 between two men
> upon the issue of slavery. Our first debater is Jacob
> Faulkner, a slave owner on a large and very old cotton and
> tobacco plantation. The property has been in his family
> for three generations, and remains prosperous. Faulkner
> owns some 175 slaves, which are housed in adequate, if
> not grand, housing.
>
> His debate opponent is one Alvin Stewart, a Kentuckian
> who by chance was my great-great grandfather. Alvin is
> not a man of great wealth. Rather, he is a subsistence
> farmer with little in the way of educational qualifications.
> He is, nonetheless, opposed to slavery, and dedicated to
> his country. The debate occurred on the front porch of a
> general store.
>
> "I understand and sympathize that you are adverse to
> the ownership of slaves", said Faulkner. "That is certainly

your right and not an unreasonable position to take, but I beg that you take a broader look at the conditions presented. These people who work for me are simply not able, without my assistance, to keep skin and bone together. Would you throw them out, like so much garbage, to scrape along as best they could? What of their children? Would you drive them off as well? Working for me is a privilege for they are housed in decent housing, I pay for their board and allow them to supplement what I give them with vegetables grown on my property by my permission. I do not beat them, nor sell them away unless conditions require it. With me, they are guaranteed a life."

"What you say is true", responded Alvin, "but it omits consideration of the fact that life on your plantation is a life without human dignity and independence. They are chattels at best and are treated as such. Do you think that is wasted on them? Do you not see that you have taken from them the nourishment of human dignity which should sustain them? The ownership of people is wrong, beyond argument, and to defend it places you in a position of defending that which is indefensible."

"Sir!" roared Squire Faulkner. "You forget yourself! I have merely stated my opinion on this most divisive of issues. You have your opinion, as I discern, but you have no right to stand in judgment of mine. I will debate you so long as the rules of civil, moderate discourse are recognized, but I will not stand for moralistic preaching from a dirt farmer such as yourself!"

Alas, the remainder of the debate is lost to history, but I believe that which was lost would not have been valuable to us in any event. These two men stood at an impasse. Squire Faulkner treated his slaves well enough, but they remained chattels, whose lives were not their own. Alvin urged that the ownership of people violated a moral imperative which the Squire did not recognize. To the Squire, there were merely two opinions, both worthy of respect. To Alvin, one of those opinions violated the laws of justice, was evil, and not worthy of respect. Alvin thus invoked the 19th Century PC Police, and the Squire resented it, bitterly.

If we are to parse this debate properly, we must acknowledge that it is deeply flawed as presented. The two men debating have no "skin in the game". The critical issues presented do not touch either for they are both white. The missing voice is that of the enslaved. To Squire Faulkner and Alvin Stewart, inclusion of this missing voice is beyond consideration. The one critical voice in the debate is forever silenced by the understanding of the time, a constraint tacitly accepted even by Alvin. The Squire and Alvin were debating words and concepts. The real issue was, and is, human lives.

What we are seeing in the Black Lives Matter demonstrations today is the reassertion of that long-silenced voice, and with it, a blow to the societal racism which has silenced it for so long. This cannot be done in a moderate way, as a sanitized debate. The hurt is too deep. Integrity demands that the debate cannot proceed without that voice. However uncomfortable, silence always benefits the oppressor. The wound, however terrible, is always to the silenced voice.

My Granny's Morphine

Miss Erma Singleton
age 16

I spent my professional life as prosecuting attorney ruining other people's lives. I told myself that that I was doing "justice" but after a lifetime, I'm still not clear on what that word means. To the extent that I was scrupulous to follow the law, I think I can say I acted "justly" but that is not the same as "doing justice" is it?

Our system of laws is designed to insure, as nearly as may be, an orderly and peaceful environment conducive to the nourishment of a just society, by imposing consequences on behaviors we wish to discourage. That's a defensible decision as there are people who must be confined for the good of all. It's also a flawed decision for we are then led to divide humanity into the "good guys" and the "bad guys". That is simply not what my experience taught me about humanity. People are much too complicated to grant validity to so crude a division.

As the epidemic of addiction grew in my little county, it became clear to me that what I was doing was actually adding harm to that which had already been touched by misery, operating on the assumption that others tempted by opioids would observe the fate of addicts and choose some other course. The data do not bear out that assumption.

The surprising truth is that my maternal grandmother, Granny Stewart, was one of them. In 1932, Granny had her gall bladder removed. In 1932, the removal of a gall bladder was not a trivial matter. They split her from stem to stern. Her recovery from surgery was painful and extended. Her doctors gave her morphine, for that was the accepted practice at the time. Granny became addicted. Thereafter, her family covertly obtained "her medicine" for her, presumably from sympathetic physicians. She lived a long life.

It doesn't take much imagination to fancy how such a situation would have been dealt with during my time as felony prosecutor. The law is clear that addictions must not be fed, no matter the reasons motivating such actions. When I first learned of Granny's addiction, I asked myself, "What harm did feeding my Granny's addiction do to society's quest for an orderly and peaceful environment conducive to the nourishment of a just society?" I could not construct a satisfactory answer.

Contrast our approach to law enforcement with that I experienced in Northern Ireland where I had gone to play music. Our hosts drove us from the Republic, across the border, guarded by armed soldiers, to Newtownards where we were to play a pub. Play we did, and a great time was had by all with the music and the excellent beer. At 9:00, the pub was required by law to close but by generally accepted convention, the landlord merely pulled down the blinds, meaning no more could be admitted and the music went on.

As we finished, I went round the corner to the snug to encounter what appeared to be the entire Newtownards' police department who had been there the whole time, enjoying the music. One officer approached and said with a big Irish smile, "Well, now, lad! You haven't been in the beer, then, have you?"

"Uh...well", I stuttered. "M..might have been. A bit..."

The officer roared with laughter. "T'is no problem, lad! We'll drive you home!"

The contrast has bedeviled me ever since. Where would we be without law, and how, other than by inflicting harm, might we enforce it? But, how can life be improved by the intentional, institutional infliction of harm? The contrast became too much for me when I was finally handed a death-qualified case. That meant that in the event of a guilty verdict it would be my job to urge the jury to return a punishment of death. Think of the consequences of such a thing! Two people had already been killed. Two more would be killed at the order of the jury. Some medical professional would have to prepare their arms for a lethal injection. Some prison guard or guards would have to deliberately deliver the condemned to the death chamber where another medical professional, sworn to see to the health of others, would have to hook the lines up to the death machine. A prison guard I would never know would be required to operate the death machine, then leave the room with the knowledge that his duty extinguished the life of another.

I couldn't do it. I just couldn't do it. The Irish policeman and my grandmother shouted at me. I told the judge I couldn't and requested that a different prosecutor's office be appointed to prosecute the case. The judge responded in disgust, "Oh shit!"

The case was tried by another Commonwealth's Attorney. A verdict of guilty was returned but the punishment was set at life in prison. The people of my community who granted mercy to the defendants then voted me out of office at the next election. My grandmother returned to her grave. The Irish policeman laughed and laughed and laughed.

My Guys

You cannot escape the phrase "systemic racism" and the emotion it evokes. Few people would be so bold as to proclaim themselves in favor of racism, but at the NFL's opening game, the Chiefs announcer called for "a moment of silence dedicated to the ongoing fight for equality" and the fans booed. I simply do not get it. Are the fans in favor of inequality, or are they simply upset by being forced to acknowledge publicly that of which we are all aware privately – we are most loyal to our own tribes?

Half a century ago, I was a university policeman. I "went 10-10" (out of service, subject to call) for my supper and stepped out of my cruiser at Jerry's on Limestone. Immediately, I heard a gunshot! I got back in my cruiser, advised dispatch of shots fired and "went 10-8" (in service) heading in the direction of the shot.

As I turned on to Upper Street, I saw a Lexington Police officer in foot pursuit of a black male. The officer pointed, and I followed his lead. The black male turned left at the railroad tracks. Those tracks ended in a 10' high wall. I drew my weapon, and ordered him to surrender, which he did, placing his hands on the wall in submission.

At this point, the LPD officer came around my right side with a stick and began beating the man on the legs and back. The man I was holding at gunpoint!

"What did he do?" I yelled.

"I don't know, but I'm going to find out", was the reply.

I turned my weapon on the officer and ordered him to stand down.

What had happened there? The officer was the only one of the two with a weapon, so it is not much of a stretch to believe that the shot I heard was from his weapon. We know from the officer's own words that he had no probable cause to believe the man had committed an offense justifying the use of deadly force, but deadly force had unquestionably been used. Neither did the LPD officer exhibit any compunction over confessing that to me – he saw blue and a badge. To him, that meant that his actions were covered. That is the earmark of tribal behavior. My tribe, right or wrong, but my tribe.

Sergeants were called. Sergeants conferred. What was the outcome? No idea. The man was taken into custody by LPD. I was never informed any further. The system covered violations motivated by race, just as the LPD officer assumed that I would do. That is why I see systemic racism as a reflection of the tribal loyalty baked into our genes from the beginning.

Would many of the fans booing at the Chiefs game have approved of the LPD officer's conduct? No, I honestly don't think that they would have done. Would they advocate for a system which fails to hold wrong-doers in blue with badges accountable for their actions? No, I honestly don't think that they would. What, then, were they booing?

Not all things which can be faced can be changed, but no affront to human dignity can be changed unless it is first faced. To do so, though, is to rock the boat of our culture, the stability in which we live. That is intensely uncomfortable and for many it is better that some should be treated inequitably, even beaten or killed than that they should be made uncomfortable and doubly so if those being treated inequitably are easily identifiable as "not one of us", a distinction made most often on the basis of race.

How does that feel to one on the receiving end? I even experienced that.

On a different night I and a friend were driving at night. We often did this to escape wives and to solve the world's problems (not that the world ever listened to us). We entered Berea and a cruiser fell in behind us. I checked my speed. Lawful. I could not imagine why he was following us except for my out-of-county license. It marked me as "not one of us".

At the city limits, he pulled us over. He ordered me out of the car. Why? Because he could, 4th Amendment be damned. I walked, as I was directed, toward his cruiser. He shoved me from behind between the shoulder blades. Why? Because he could. I was "not one of us". I could not complain.

In the car, he started filling out a Field Interrogation Form. He was going to officially mark me as a suspicious outsider.

Name?

Occupation?

"Police officer", I replied. "And the guy in the car is a reporter for the Associated Press. Your ass pretty much belongs to me now." I was mad! I'm not proud of that, but I was mad!

In the mind of the Lexington officer who was beating my prisoner and that of the Berea officer all of God's creation could be divided into "my guys" and "other guys". "My guys" are to be respected. "Other guys" are to be viewed with suspicion as potential threats to "my guys".

The Berea officer knew that as an outsider, a judge would reject my account in favor of whatever charge he would choose to place. His team would stick together, and he knew that it would. My reply told him that the light of truth would shine upon what had happened and he panicked and fled. My sin, though, is that my argument was directed to the question, "Who has the power here now?" rather than to the actual question, "Why do you abuse the small power you have been given?" I am ashamed.

The news is filled with discussions of strategies for improving police training and organization, but as has been noted, culture eats strategy for breakfast. No officer I ever spoke with, including me, was ever taught a choke hold, yet cities are now banning choke holds. Their heart is in the right place, but their efforts are in the wrong direction. What is needed is a cultural shift, not strategic tinkering.

What would have happened in Minneapolis if one or more of the rookies (the one with only 4 shifts under his belt, perhaps?) had tried to intervene against his training officer? What would have happened if a rookie pointed his service weapon at the senior officer and ordered him to stand down? What would have happened if the rookies, together, pulled the training officer off of George Floyd? Would the administration have supported such an action if George Floyd had survived? Without the raised public awareness resulting from George Floyd's death, would the rookies have survived the administration's review? I rather think not.

These are the issues which must be addressed – the cultural embrace of "my guys, right or wrong" and the certainty of violence as the only effective answer to societal problems. We have dipped our tongues into slaughter and learned well the taste of it. We have to get this right if we are to ever call ourselves civilized people.

No Man Knows

When I was a young father, my son demanded that we install a swimming pool.

"I can't afford a swimming pool, my son", I replied.

"They don't cost anything!" he stubbornly insisted. "You just dig a hole and paint it blue."

Well, to a five year old, that makes perfect sense. He simply did not know the extent of his own ignorance. Therefore, a simple explanation which led to the outcome he desired was perfectly acceptable. Such is the case with all of us, I would submit. The wisest thing ever told me was, "No man knows what he does not know" and its corollary, "The less a man knows, the more convinced he becomes of his own omniscience". This obvious, but too often overlooked, wisdom bears on much of the turmoil in which we live. We long for simple solutions to the distressing events which fill the news and our desire blinds us to the depths of our own ignorance. To end disorder in the streets, you just put more police or the National Guard on the streets, perhaps with fixed bayonets, and show these punks who's boss.

As it happened, I participated in just such an experiment – the Vietnam protests at the University of Kentucky. I was a University Police Officer. The protesters damaged property – they burnt at least one building. The National Guard, yes, with fixed bayonets as I recall, were called out. The stage was set for another tragic confrontation. This time, though, our commanders ordered us to patrol the area between the students and the Guard, doing what we could to keep the groups apart. Our commanders recognized that there were forces worthy of fear abroad, both in the protests and in the state's possible responses. Our orders were designed to keep the University community from finding out just how lethal the forces represented there might be. We were successful. No one died.

We are less successful today. Order must be restored at any cost, we think, and the simple way to do that is through violence and arms. As Walter Wink noted,

> **The belief that violence "saves" is so successful because it doesn't seem to be mythic in the least. Violence simply appears to be the nature of things. It's what works.** [2]

Those who believe in the power of violence to offer salvation have blinded themselves to the depth of feeling which is being expressed in the protests. You just dig a hole and paint it blue, you see.

Race educator Jane Eliot told an auditorium full of people,

> **I want every white person in this room who would be happy to be treated as this society, in general, treats our citizens – our black citizens – if you, as a white person, would be happy to receive the same treatment as our black citizens do in this society, please stand.** [3]

No one stood. That's damning. It is not only our ignorance of the anger which drives the protests that leads us to accept simple solutions leading to outcomes which we desire. It is a willful blinding of ourselves to the inequities suffered by American citizens of color. These protests demand that "All men are created equal" be more than just a slogan.

Not all things which can be faced can be changed, but nothing may be changed without facing up to it. We must face up to the sin of racism which has tainted our great country for too long and join with our brothers and sisters in healing.

---

[2] Facing the Myth of Redemptive Violence, Walter Wink
[3] https://www.youtube.com/watch?v=1mcCLm_LwpE&app=desktop

The Preacher
Receives a Sermon

I had finished delivering a sermon based in part on this too-often overlooked passage from the book of Job:

> The Lord answered Job out of the whirlwind:
> "Who is this that darkens counsel by words without
>   knowledge?
> Gird up your loins like a man,
>   I will question you, and you shall declare to me.
> "Where were you when I laid the foundation of the
>   earth?

I had droned on in my usual didactic fashion, dwelling on the point that as mere mortals we should be wary of getting above ourselves. I thought I had done a workmanlike enough job, but at the close of the service, one of the congregations, a man of great learning, came to speak to me about the difficulties restaurants are experiencing in finding people to "wait tables".

"They just don't want to work", he told me.

I'm sure my reply cast no light into the darkness, but his comment lit me up. When we encounter a situation which displeases us, our first inclination is to identify the guilty party, then to deal with that guilty party appropriately, quite apart from the underlying situation. Five million deaths world-wide and we are still trying to determine if the Corona virus originated in a lab in China as if that is the first priority. For us humans, it IS of the first priority. We NEED to identify the guilty party. Worse, we need to imagine that it is within our power to define good and evil. Pope Francis spoke in my head.

> **"Adam, where are you?" (cf. Gen 3:9). Where are you, o man? What have you come to? ...Who corrupted you? Who disfigured you? Who led you to presume that you are the master of good and evil? Who convinced you that you were god? Not only did you torture and kill your brothers and sisters, but you sacrificed them to yourself, because you made yourself a god. [4]**

To the American understanding, work leads to self-sufficiency. Conversely, refusal to work shouts of a shattered soul who wishes to be only a burden to others. Ergo, we have our guilty party.

Not so fast there, Preacher. Not so fast. If conditions have been arranged such that work does not lead to self-sufficiency, the rules of the game have been changed. The sucking noise one can hear if one will but listen is the consolidation of wealth into few hands at the expense of many. Finding people to work for ten bucks an hour is difficult not because the people who might have filled those jobs are too lazy to work (however pleasant that sounds to those of us fortunate enough to have a living wage job) but because, for many, the demands of life, including child care, make it impossible.

I have been taught.

---

[4] Pope Francis, 26 May 2014

Prowling for Villains

Today, a life-long friend posted a meme asking,

"Did you know that they brought Rioters in Busses to Kenosha to burn buildings and riot?"

That seemed to me to be an extraordinary thing to assert, particularly given the spelling errors, and I asked, "Why do you think this is accurate?" The reply was, "They've done it before."

I was intrigued, and asked, "Why do you think THAT is accurate? I'm seeking the evidence upon which you are relying." His response was, "I'm on my way to work and I'm not in court. It's my opinion." I answered, "I see" and our conversation ended. Does this not sound singular to you, or am I prowling for villains again?

In the best of all possible worlds, "opinion" should mean a conclusion reached after careful evaluation of available evidence. My sense is that the contemporary definition is closer to "my preferred way of perceiving the world" or "a perspective which makes me feel righteous". Not to repeat myself, but it might also mean, "My tribe's holy Scripture". I don't think this applies only to those on the right. I think this is a human problem, requiring a unified human examination.

We don't think at all of a "need for villains" but that need seems to underlay much of our behavior. Imagine, for a minute, a monastery filled with devout monks. It is an orderly community, each brother going about his assigned tasks with diligence. Now, imagine that Batman moves in. What is the first thing Batman requires in order to fulfill himself? Is it not a villain? Where in the peaceful community would he find such a thing? Realistically, his choices are only two: create a villain or abandon his very identity and purpose for being. The human choice is to create a villain. No one happily and willingly abandons his very identity and purpose for being. Such a thing is just not in us.

So, my friend has focused on those who riot and burn buildings. Such things are evil and wrong, agreed, but look at his language. "Did you know that THEY brought Rioters in Busses to Kenosha to burn buildings and riot?" "THEY'VE done it before."

Who is "THEY"? The villains. The ones he opposes, and he is not alone. The responses to his posting were heavy with suggestions of what might beneficially be done to "them", and the suggestions were pretty brutal. I went back to copy them and my friend has deleted them. I'm proud of him.

Focusing on the destruction of property, rather than on the cause of the anger, gives those who do so permission to feel righteous, for what righteous person would approve of such thing? Yet that focus blinds us to the context from which that anger arises.

It seems hard wired into our human souls to erect tribal totems in whose presence we feel so secure that we can dance naked around them. Of course, we 21st Century people are much too sophisticated to call them "totems". We call them "opinions" but we nevertheless dance naked around them stripped of any real evidence which might intervene between us and our opinion.

Unruly

There was a report on the news of an uptick in "unruly" passengers" on airplanes. My attention immediately went to the word "unruly". It's hardly used today except to describe airline passengers who decide that 30,000 feet in the air would be a good place to pick a fight with an airline attendant over whether or not to wear a mask, but when you look at the word, "unruly", you begin to see something more to it. An unruly person is one who refuses to be bound by rules. "I have rights! Constitutional rights! You can't infringe upon my rights by your rules!"

Such a person is an anarchist and that should end the debate, but of course it does not. We have somehow come to accept that there is high moral ground behind the position of the unruly. There is not. We live within community and owe responsibility for the welfare of the community which supports us. The unruly among us blind themselves to those responsibilities as the price of raising the individual back to a status which, it is felt, has been stolen from them. They act, it seems to me, from existential fear – fear that they will be erased by the forces which govern our complex communities. To one suffering from such an existential fear, ascent to even common sense health advice in the midst of a world-wide pandemic seems but the beginning of a slippery slope to extinction.

We must devise strategies to allay those fears which drive irrational behaviors.

Port of Ashland

We lunched at the Port of Ashland again, watching the Ohio River drain its portion of the continent. My eyes went to the geese. There is a healthy flock of Canadian Geese living at Port of Ashland. Animals, by nature or design, are either prey or predators. Prey animals tend to have eyes on the sides of their heads so that they can spot an attack from any direction. Predators tend to have eyes in the front, granting them binocular vision to more accurately mount an attack. Geese are prey; people are predators.

Nothing at all surprising about that until you take the time to really look at the scene at Port of Ashland. The predators got out of their vehicles and, instead of hunting the geese, they were sharing their food with the prey animals. Even more astonishing (for geese are not generally credited with subtle minds) the geese were gathered around the predators, accepting the food, laying aside their natural fear. The design of evolution was turned upon its head, and there were no unpleasant consequences by reason of that.

Our present political environment puts our predatory nature on full display. Without an easily identified and real adversary we have turned upon ourselves for to imagine life without a foe is unthinkable to our nature. Yet, the geese and the people at Port of Ashland manage to behave outside their natures. Why can we not? I would submit that we cannot for the meal is toxic.

In the current environment, Democrats would have to grant a mantle of reasonableness to the view that was no insurrection on January 6 and the insurrectionists who so injured Officer Fanone and others were tourists. Further, despite countless reviews, both political and judicial, to the contrary the 2020 election was rigged and Donald Trump is the rightful president.

Republicans would have to embrace the assertion that our democratic processes which have served us so well for 245 years once again served us well. Joe Biden was duly elected and is the lawful president. BLM has nothing to do with anything political, but is a long-delayed plea for repentance. There is no "deep state" nor any evidence of any election fraud. Perhaps most importantly, the Democrats cannot offer respect to the Republican view for it is founded in "the big lie" and such a thing precludes compromise.

Republicans do not oppose Democrats nor Democrats oppose Republicans over policy differences. Each party opposes the other for the other is prey. We are engaged in a sort of civil war, testing whether this nation, or any nation so conceived and so dedicated, can long endure. The peril has not been so great since 1860. That cry of the wolf within us will not yield to logic or evidence. It is too broad in our very DNA. To exist without an adversary is impossible to imagine. I weep for us. We appear to be dumber than geese.

The Golden Calf

There is much to fear in the present time, and the fear is great in me. The group which characterizes itself as "Conservative" have met upon a stage shaped like a Nazi uniform collar button, and they have no shame in it. As happened before, they have molded an idol of their estimate of their own righteousness and worshiped it because it is the work of their own hands, worthy of worship.

And the Lord said to Moses,

> "Go, get down! For your people whom you brought out of the land of Egypt have corrupted themselves. They have turned aside quickly out of the way which I commanded them. They have made themselves a molded calf, and worshiped it and sacrificed to it".

The people celebrate the golden calf they have made, and dance before it for they have formed their righteousness of their wealth, the very gold of their rings, and find approval there.

> So it was, as soon as he came near the camp, that he saw the calf and the dancing. So Moses' anger became hot, and he cast the tablets out of his hands and broke them at the foot of the mountain...And Moses said to Aaron, "What did this people do to you that you have brought so great a sin upon them?"
>
> So Aaron said, "Do not let the anger of my lord become hot. You know the people, that they are set on evil....

Indeed, it can never be a question of evil unless all agree upon a standard with which to measure evil, yet this simple exercise evades us. We replace the standard of righteousness we might embrace with our yearned-for validation of our own righteousness assuring us success and depriving others of a path to righteousness. By this means we assure a future of hatred and strife.

Peace Without Justice

An acquaintance posted a cut-and-paste meme expressing those topics of which he was "sick", closing with,

> **"I am sick of blaming the world for the sins of a few. I am sick of the people who are out there jumping on the bandwagon just to spread hatred, and start riots, looting & destroying other's properties."**

Naturally, with an invitation like that, I "jumped on the bandwagon" and took issue with his statement.

> **"You are telling me that you want peace. But peace without justice is not peace."**

I cannot, personally, accept the notion that these issues which hammer upon our consciousness with such insistence spring from the malice of "the people who are out there jumping on the bandwagon just to spread hatred". Neither can I accept the idea that such people are motivated by a desire to start riots and to loot stores and businesses. Neither pettiness nor individual criminality is an engine large enough to explain what we are seeing in our culture. There is a cry of pain behind the disturbing images. Justice demands that we engage that cry but to do so diverts our attention from things which are more enjoyable, things like the imagined motivation of those who issue these insistent calls for justice. However sympathetic I may be, eventually I need to look to my own interests and that may best be done by discounting the inequities before me. We are, it seems to me, both lazy and selfish by nature.

Here's an idle thought: I have never been a sports fan. I just don't enjoy sports. Speaking as an outsider, it seems to me that it is very easy, almost trivial, to be a fan of UK ball. One does not have to train, nor do wind sprints, nor run plays in inclement weather, nor subject one's self to any sort of discipline. One merely declares oneself a fan, attends the games when convenient, immersing oneself in a crowd of like believers which lifts you up when things go well, and supports you when they don't.

Could it be that this understanding actually has come to define our approach to the responsibilities of living within a democratic republic, ostensibly operated by the judgment of the many for the protection of all? A friend remarked once that people are like water – they follow the course of least resistance to a place of repose. Is it our preference to seek only a place of personal repose?

I earnestly hope not. I want to believe in the notions upon which this country was founded. I want to believe that, if given the power to govern ourselves, we will, in fact, devote ourselves to this most sacred duty. And devotion demands that we be aware of the issues and deliberately engage them. There can be no sitting in the stands cheering. We must, each of us, do the hard work, wind sprints and all.

There are people in our world who are dying and there are those who will not wear masks to protect them. Justice demands that we take note of that. There are those who have lesser lives than others because of the color of their skin or their national origin. Justice demands that we speak to that. The party of Lincoln is in danger of becoming something dark. Justice demands that its voice be restored from the forces which seek to abduct it.

I hear you when you say that you are sick to death of hearing this constant drumbeat of issues, that you want some peace in which to enjoy your life, but the sound you hear is that of justice's demands. Take comfort in these words from Common Prayer: A Liturgy for Ordinary Radicals.

Peace is not just about the absence of conflict; it's also about the presence of justice. ... A counterfeit peace exists when people are pacified or distracted or so beat up and tired of fighting that all seems calm. But true peace does not exist until there is justice, restoration, forgiveness.

I could put it no better than did one of my teachers, Rev. Dr. Lisa Davison, who began at the beginning and laid the foundation:

In Genesis 1, we hear that the Divine ru'ach ("breath") hovered over the waters of creation, and it was with that Divine ru'ach that the Holy spoke every part of creation into existence. In Genesis 2, we read that it was the Divine ru'ach of life that animated the first human, and it became a nephesh ("living being"). [5]

The Divine breath still hovers over all creation, keeping primordial chaos in check. It is the source of creativity, yearning, and connectivity within and among humans. The Divine breath is that which endows us with personality, energy, passion, wisdom, empathy, and humor. It is what makes us who we are as unique people. Without it, we would not exist. Since all humans (and all living beings) have the Divine breath within them, we are all connected. We are all distinctive and united. We are remarkable and have inherent worth. When we deprive a child of the Holy of breath, we extinguish a reflection of the Divine. The whole human family is diminished, and the Divine weeps.

It is with that same ru'ach that those who are pressed down and harmed by racism lament and protest. Those of us in positions of privilege must listen to them and heed the breath of the Holy within us to demand justice, to hold those with authority (and ourselves) accountable, and to work for a day when all children of the Holy can breathe in the fullness of the Divine Shalom.

---

[5] Facebook comment by Rev. Dr. Lisa Davison

Norm and the Whale

Norm was a wonderful old man, a beloved regular at Starbuck's and friend of all the ladies there. At his funeral, in fact, one of the baristas pinned a Starbuck's pin to his lapel. His forte was the telling of stories, and this is one of my favorites.

It happened as he was serving on a Navy ship. A pod of whales began swimming with his ship, as whales sometimes do. One of the ensigns, who had left his brains on a hook somewhere on board, came to the conclusion that it would be amusing to shoot one of the whales. Arming himself, he proceeded to do just that.

Leviathan, detecting something like a mosquito bite, stopped and turned, facing the US Navy ship holding the offender. With a flip of his tail, he charged the ship, striking the sonar equipment hanging below the keel, and bending it flat against the ship's hull. On the other side, the whale breached, raised his mighty head and proclaimed, basso profundo, "Your move, sucker".

The ship was out of service an extended period of time.

It strikes me that we would be well-advised to heed the sermon of the whale, particularly when living through times such as these. It is mid-November and 70 degrees here. California has been on fire for months and the ice sheets are melting. Your move, sucker.

My Grandfather's House

Forest Avenue was where my grandfather Schneider lived. The house looks today exactly as it did then, as if Granddad's insistence on order and design had somehow become part of the genetics of the house. Granddad was German and methodical as only Germans can be. In his workshop in the basement, there was a board with the outline of every tool painted upon it. A tool used was to be replaced on its image on the board. Beneath the garage was his yard tool storage, similarly laid out. So strict was the regimentation that we boys touched his things gingerly, if at all.

Upstairs was much the same. The living room was decorated with fragile things which were not to be touched. The furniture, apart from his chair and hers, was upholstered in horse hair which would give you a rash were you so rash as to lie upon it. In this household, things were orderly. To this day, when I pass it, I give it scarcely a glance. It offers absolutely no emotional connection to me.

Our house, on Valley Drive, was much the same. Mom was a meticulous housekeeper. Breakfast was at 7, all around the table; supper was at 6, likewise arranged. I read comic books to avoid interacting with my family, and my brother refused to eat anything put before him. Otherwise, all was orderly. Except for Dad's shop. It was a tiny space and despite occasional fits of orderliness, it was generally pretty chaotic, with tools everywhere. We boys played there with the tools. Miraculously, no one suffered grievous injury. Again, when I drive past my boyhood home, I seldom glance at it. It, too, offers me no emotional connection whatsoever.

At the top of Prospect Hill, though, matters were decidedly different. This is where my grandfather Stewart lived, in a two-story brick home some 102 years old. Interestingly, as time passed, it did not get older. It was perpetually 102 years old. Family history insisted that Granddad's house was the second brick house in Ashland, built of bricks made in ovens constructed on site. In the side yard were two enormous walnuts which had stood there since the Cherokee claimed the land. On summer afternoons, we sat beneath one and ate watermelon, and marveled at the rusted crank bucket pump from the "cistern", a brick lined chamber below, which once communicated with the gutters of the handsome old house, providing wash water. Here, at last, was some history, some romance.

The house commanded a view of Prospect Hill and was, at one time, a grand place. Entrance through the front door (which was rarely used) led into a great hall, floored in large black and white tiles. To the left, a staircase ascended, hugging the walls, to the second floor. Ahead, a hallway led to what must have been the back of the house. To the right was what once was the parlor. To the left was the doorway to the apartment my grandparents lived in, for by the time I knew the place, it had become four apartments. My grandparents lived in one. His son and family occupied the top floor and the remaining two were rented out.

Passing by Prospect Hill, the modern home which replaced Granddad's house is, for me, a jarring sight. The owners of the modern house have felled one of the walnuts, older than our country. Perhaps it blocked their view? Neither can I bear to look at the tiny footprint representing Granddad's shop. Granddad's shop! The Smithsonian's museums held nothing to compare with Granddad's shop. Where Granddad Schneider's sterile workshop promised productivity but offered only organization, Granddad Stewart's shop was organic. It grew like kudzu. When he finished with a screwdriver, he was likely to toss it over his shoulder and, after his passing, we found rafts of screwdrivers covering the floor. His tools were rusted, a part of the history of the place, and because of that were infused with the same romance and history which formed the structure of his 102 year old house. This is what drew us boys to Granddad's shop. Here we could watch Granddad work, something we truly never saw Granddad Schneider do. That would have disturbed the regularity of his system, but Granddad Stewart used his tools and we boys watched.

As I passed by, Stan Rogers came on the music, playing "Last Watch" a song of the end of a proud old ship, now gone to salvage. He sang of the salvagers quenching the fires beneath her boilers, and I remembered the descendants of the proud iron men who founded this area feeding the remains of Bellefonte furnace into the maw of Amanda furnace, then remembered the cooling of Amanda, and the reassuring talk that the hearth was still warm, and might one day again blast. Amanda is dead and cold, an obscene skeleton.

When I pass the site of Granddad's house, though I cannot appreciate the modern house, I wonder, is the cistern still there, beneath a porch or patio? Could it still communicate with long-gone gutters of another time as I seem to do in my wanderings? Stan Rogers sings of the end of things, and we live that. If he can stand it, I can as well. I wonder: Who now is left to melt Amanda Furnace?

I Come and Stand at Every Door

I am twice blessed, and I want to share it. My iPhone was playing random music to my car sound system and decided I needed to hear "I Come and Stand at Every Door" by Nâzım Hikmet Ran, sung by Ann Wells. The character to which Ann gave voice is a seven year old victim of the bomb we dropped on Hiroshima. She sings:

> "I come and stand at every door
> But none can hear my silent tread.
> I knock and yet remain unseen
> For I am dead, for I am dead."
> "I'm only seven though I died
> In Hiroshima long ago
> I'm seven now as I was then
> When children die, they do not grow."
> "My hair was scorched by swirling flames,
> My eyes grew dim, my eyes grew blind
> Death came and turned my bones to dust
> And that was scattered by the wind"

I can see that little girl as clearly as I can see anything in my world. A little girl, just seven. How could a country built on such high principles embark upon such an obscenity? Don't you dare recite to me the rationalizations I've heard all my life for what we did! Those rationalizations will not dry my tears. They will only show me how adept we are at constructing convincing reasons to do wrong. I am so ashamed for I am reminded of the words of 1 John.

> "If we say that we have no sin, we deceive ourselves, and the truth is not in us. If we confess our sins, he who is faithful and just will forgive us our sins and cleanse us from all unrighteousness. If we say that we have not sinned, we make him a liar, and his word is not in us." [6]

Even now, typing these lines, my eyes are filled with tears. I, who sometimes cannot find the emotional resources for my grandchildren, am now overwhelmed by the lines of a song. I wept in empathy for that child and when the song concluded, I played it again and wept harder.

My second blessing came that evening as Henry L. Gates searched for Mandy Patinkin's roots and I went along.

Mandy knew little beyond his immediate family, but Dr. Gates is not so slight a researcher. He followed Mandy's family and was able to place his family in a Polish shtetl. A shtetl, of course was a small town with a large Ashkenazi Jewish population which existed in Central and Eastern Europe before the Holocaust. Mandy's eyes grew wider. Then we heard of the authorities coming in the evening, ordering the entire population to be at their front doors in the morning with their belongings. They were loaded onto carts. From the carts to a train. From the train to Treblinka to the ovens and the crematoria, all of them, men and women separately. The dam burst for Mandy and for me. I lost no family in the Holocaust. He didn't know he had and we wept great tears, the both of us.

Yes, I was not taught about love and empathy as a child. It was not done in my family. My family was satisfied if the children learned propriety and inoffensiveness. Yes, it left a mark upon me but with Ann Wells and Mandy Patinkin I have opened the dam, however slightly, and I go to my knees in gratitude.

Confess, oh America! Confess and repent.

---

[6] 1 John 1:8-10 NRSV

The McCreary Building

We children of the 50's and 60's grew up understanding the United States as a foundational bulwark. We never considered how short a period of history we encompass. That is what came to mind during lunch at the restaurant at the hotel. We were on the balcony and that put us close to the top of the McCreary Building across the street. Its facade informed us that it was built in 1907, 113 years ago.

I graduated from high school in 1964. One hundred thirteen years before that, just one McCreary earlier than my high school graduation, was 1851. The great civil war, testing whether this nation, or any nation so conceived and so dedicated, can long endure was still 9 years in the future.

One hundred thirteen years before that was 1738. We had no country. We were a colony. Only two McCrearies before my high school graduation Kentucky was a howling wilderness.

There is a current hypothesis called "the Silurian hypothesis" which reflects upon the possibility that there might have been an advanced civilization here on earth millions of McCrearies ago, whose presence has been so thoroughly obliterated by the passage of time that it can no longer be detected. There is no evidence of such a civilization, but absence of evidence, as it is said, is not evidence of absence. What if we are not the big shots we imagine ourselves to be? What if an undetected blip on the graph of time is really our highest attainment?

Our country, flawed as it is, began a great experiment less than two McCrearies ago to determine whether a country founded on high-sounding and abstract principles could long prevail. In this time of political chaos, it is up to us to answer that question as we did in 1861. Let us hope we are up to the challenge. I am frankly not optimistic. Abstract principles do not play well with deprivations and frustrations imposed by an unfeeling world which sees humanity as merely the plowed furrows from which profit is harvested.

Have we any McCrearies left to us or are we as dead and forgotten to history as the Silurians?

Mandrake the Magician

When I was a child, Sunday meant church, an obligation to be endured through the inevitable lunch at the Chimney Corner, following which I was finally free to pursue my own interests. That included, first and foremost, the Funny Papers. Each Sunday the Ashland Daily Independent produced a magnum opus of a newspaper which included the comics. I always saved Mandrake the Magician for last.

A case can be made, I'm told, in favor of the proposition that Mandrake the Magician was the first superhero. Mandrake was a stage magician, but he was gifted with the power to "gesture hypnotically" and make the bad guys see things that weren't really there. Not only to see them, but to make them real enough for his targets to alter their behavior. A miscreant might be running from a policeman but Mandrake would "gesture hypnotically" and the criminal would believe he had run right into a wall, and stop.

Yes, as time went on and I grew wiser in the ways of the world, Mandrake's power to implant seemingly real perceptions in the minds of miscreants wore a bit thin. Eventually, I even outgrew the Funny Papers and went on to more sophisticated undertakings. Generally involving girls. Generally, disappointing.

A conversation I had with a long time, but not close, acquaintance brought Mandrake to mind. She had posted something on Facebook that defended Donald Trump, lifting him to be but slightly lower than the savior of mankind. I simply could not understand how anyone, much less a woman, would hold such a position and foolishly pried into it, suggesting that defending the indefensible in public would not persuade anyone, but would make her look foolish. "How can you defend a man who thinks that his fame entitles him to grab women by the p___y?"

Her response astonished me. Not only did she accuse me of being a "pussy" because I would not write out the word, but she said that should Trump do such a thing to her, she would be "honored". Donald had gestured hypnotically and made her see what he wills. More than that, he had somehow made her find objectively offensive behavior "honorable".

You and I know there are no such things as witches, but elderly ladies were nonetheless burnt at the stake in Salem. You and I know that George Takai and his family were no threat to the United States but they and some 120,000 other United States citizens were relocated behind barbed wire during World War II. The verdict finding former policeman Derek Chauvin guilty of murder in the death of George Floyd marks the point, I earnestly hope, at which we stop paying attention to cultural hypnotic gestures and get on with the business of forging one nation with liberty and justice for all. Foundational principles which cease to be foundational also cease to be principles.

Low Grade Depression

Like Michelle Obama, I suffer from low grade depression. Well, "suffer" is probably too strong a term. I am inconvenienced by low grade depression. I'm sad most of the time. I have lost interest in those things which once gave me joy. The truth is that I haven't touched my harps since I was honored to be asked to appear on a recording with the 1937 Flood, an act of such supreme kindness that it took my breath away. As things stand now, I no longer remember which end of the harp to blow into.

It's the quarantine, of course. It has taken from me the routines and community in which I so comfortably lived, and left me with an aching emptiness in their place. It hasn't been misery, understand. Kathy and I are so compatible that we have been able to find routines of mutual interest to pass away the time, but it is indisputable that the loss of my accustomed way of life has caused me pain, and that my body's response to that pain has brought on an intractable low grade depression. I desperately want my life to be restored, but see no way that might be accomplished so long as the virus strides the land. The need for change is undeniable.

When I look about our community now, I see people who are placed, by virtue of videos showing undeniable evidence of wrong-doing by those we should be able to trust, in untenable positions. The unquestionable truths taught us from before time began for us are shown to be alloyed with the cruelty and human mistakes we were never taught to engage. The good guys are shown to be more guy than good, subject to errors of judgment like the rest of us. The bad guys we were taught to fear are shown to be human like the rest of us, with families who love them. Most of all, the terrible error of sorting the good guys from the bad guys on skin color, bred into us from the beginning, is shown for the awful sin it is. Is it any wonder that we weep?

I passed an impressive house in an impressive neighborhood today. In front was a Trump sign. Over the Trump sign was the notice, "We vote pro-life". Whoever owns that house did not come to own it by being poorly-educated or lacking in accomplishment. We can't write off his support for this terribly damaged man on that basis. What we can do is to ask why he does not engage the question of his support? Is the anti-abortion sentiment the fig leaf he hides his awareness behind? Is he by nature a racist who wishes to find a more acceptable justification for supporting a racist president?

Or is it more a case of the pain that change inevitably causes each of us as we are forced, by contagion or circumstances, to give up our accustomed communities, the communities from which we have gained strength and identity, for the good of strangers we have habitually excluded from our consciousness? I'm not wise enough to answer that, but it may offer something to think about. It is time and past time to engage the fullness of the meaning of "the family of God".

Long Street

This past year has been an experiential adaptation to age and my disease. I'm really quite grateful for it, though the intervention of quarantine and the associated inconveniences necessitated by the virus have been trying. The time has now come to examine my strategies for age adaptation, and how they have evolved.

Think of a younger, more active person who reveled in running, jumping, competitions and physical activities. Now, imagine that, through no fault of his own, he is injured and can no longer engage in the activities which gave him so much joy previously. Worse yet, as a result of his injury, he must now wear orthopedic shoes which grant him a measure of independence, in that he can still walk, but which deny him the activities he had so enjoyed. I think the very human thing would be to let those within his community know of his pain and seek comfort from those around him. But what form would that comfort take? That has been my question this year. What I'm looking for is our societal response to the inevitability of age.

The advice I received from many was that since age and infirmity is inevitable, find the happiness left to you and focus on that. Certainly, there is wisdom there, but for me it is an unsatisfying wisdom for it counsels that the best way to confront the limitations of age and infirmity is to be careful never to confront the limitations of age and infirmity. That doesn't work for me. Something new has come into my life – vascular dementia – and I need to get to know it. I can't do that by taking up stamp collecting or some other such distraction. If I must wear orthopedic shoes, I want to know the limits of orthopedic shoes. This would be a helpful time for the universe to intervene with a useful suggestion. The universe did.

I took my mother-in-law to have her "hair did". I waited in the parking lot on the corner of 13th and Long Street. Now, for those who don't live here, Long Street isn't. It is a street which tried, unsuccessfully, to live out its optimistic name, but is cut in several places so that it is impossible to travel from one end to the other without going someplace which isn't Long Street. In the case of the portion near me, Long Street leaves 13th Street at a steep downward angle for about two blocks, then dead ends. It has been that way for so long that a stairway up and down the incline permitting people to climb up and board the street car still exists.

From my perch on the parking lot cantilevered over the hillside down which Long Street goes, I could see all the way to the dead end and began thinking that for Long Street and my time on earth the end is in sight. I then fancied how useless a dead end street, like my mind, is, for it allows no transit. Neither Long Street nor I have any place to go. At this point in my ruminations, a car stopped on 13th Street with his left turn signal on. I looked with considerable consternation. Where did he think he was going? Long Street is a dead end. Nevertheless, when traffic cleared he descended Long Street!

"Huh!", I thought.

Soon, a motorcycle did the same, waiting for traffic to clear to allow him, as well, to follow Long Street to its anticlimactic end in the woods which separate this portion of Long Street from the next portion. I was frankly puzzled. The drivers of two vehicles had now inconvenienced themselves to deliberately travel a dead-end road. As I watched several more vehicles, including a large van, descended Long Street, and some ascended. There was two-way traffic on a dead-end road. I was fascinated, fascinated enough to leave my car and go to the back of the parking lot and watch.

Of course, there was no mystery at all. There are several houses on this portion of Long Street. It was nearing supper time, and I was seeing the occupants of those houses coming home at the end of the work day. The epiphany I was searching for was being played out in front of me. These drivers were living their lives just as they would have done, Long Street or no Long Street. They were not distracting themselves by considering the plain end of the road before them. They were coming home in anticipation of supper.

It may well be that the secret to a life well-lived is to simply live it. It may well be that the secret to living with orthopedic shoes is to embrace them fully. Mind where you place your focus.

Lonely Old Man

The other curse of outliving your usefulness is loneliness. We are built to live within community. It is as necessary to us as food and water. Our community, our web of friends and acquaintances, is the nursery which sustains us, no matter how grown up we become. When life serves up a celebration, it is our friends and acquaintances to whom we turn to share our gladness. When life serves up the death of a loved one, a fatal diagnosis, a broken marriage, it is to these same friends and acquaintances that we turn for the support we need to live through the horror.

As we age, we see our community shrink. Old friends die or move away. Other friends, once pillars of support, can no longer be such because of their own infirmities. Still others have lost interest in the topics which once bound you together and so drift away to pursue new interests. It is inevitable that as we age and become more burdensome that we should hear from even life-long friends that you, as you now are, are of less importance to them than they are to you. They find, as it were, that they are done with the conversation that defined the friendship earlier.

Yes, that is sad, but, as I noted, it is inevitable, and not malicious. As the years press upon me, I have had to give up a number of long friendships. It hurts. It hurts a lot, but the alternative, pretending to keep the friendship alive while I become more and more of an obligation, a burden, would be more painful yet.

I go my way alone, with regrets, of course, but also with pride that when I stumble, it is only my knees which are skinned. I go in pride that I have not become a burden to another.

The World We Live In

Talk To The Chicken

Recent events have turned my thoughts to the loss of personal potency. There was a time, and it seems not too long ago, when commercial transactions occurred "man to man". That is, vendor and customer dealt with each other as they stood, rather than as a representative of a faceless corporate power and its natural prey. With age, however, I have discovered that I had, and have, no more power to affect the complexities of the real world than has a hummingbird the power to affect the directions of the wind. The world I now inhabit is designed to rub my nose in my impotence. It was not always so, and I mourn the loss.

Case in point: our refrigerator failed. I went to a big box store to replace it. In the store, I was a customer in need with a thousand dollars in his pocket. I was welcomed with all courtesy as a lion might welcome a lamb.

I chose from among the models shown me, but was told that the ice maker was a separate purchase. Nonetheless, I was promised delivery of the ice maker in three weeks. The refrigerator, itself, was to be installed the next day. I left my money on their assurance and went home. This was the point at which things went off the rails for by treating me well, they had extracted my thousand dollars, the only part of me in which they had any interest. Had I been a farmer's field, the harvest had been made and the bare soil held no further interest to them.

The day of delivery came and the refrigerator was placed in my kitchen but then we were told that the old refrigerator, which had an ice maker, was connected to the water supply and that they "couldn't cut copper".

"What do you propose to do about that?", I asked.

"Nothing. We're done.", and with that, they left me with two refrigerators in my small kitchen. I dialed the big box store and demanded to speak to a manager. That's what old people say when they're mad.

A voice I estimated to belong to a 20-something woman came on the line. I told her my story. Her answer was, "We don't do the deliveries, so we're not responsible."

Here we have the punchline. "You silly man! We've already harvested your money! What are you going to do? Tell me you'll never shop here again? We could carry our profit/loss sheet to 18 decimal places and never notice." And she is right. I'm powerless and impotent to insist on fair treatment from so gigantic a machine. I am gravel beneath its feet.

In the world in which I was born, a merchant who did not deliver on his end of the deal would make it right. If I bought a dozen eggs from the grocer and found three rotten, I would take it back and the grocer would make it good. Not so the big box store. "You'll need to talk to the chicken." We're done with you.

Eventually, I hired a plumber to "cut the copper" and the big box store sent out the same people to "install" the new refrigerator. That is to say they removed the old one, reversed the door of the new one and pushed it back into its place.

It wasn't until three weeks later (still no ice maker) that we found what "install" means. The refrigerator began rocking. It was clearly not leveled. Back I went, demanding again to speak to the manager for that is what older people say. While waiting I said to another customer, "Run. Run away" in front of a salesman. He snickered. Not only am I impotent, all customers are impotent.

We customers, when faced with leviathan, have no leverage. Talk to the chicken is the best we're going to get.

To my great surprise the manager, a man closer to my age, had grown from the same soil as had I. He followed me to my house, retrieved the incorrectly installed leveling foot, leveled the refrigerator and left amid handshakes.

I am so grateful to that man, but I'm also aware that he was going against company policy. He was supposed to send me to the chicken. I had been harvested. There was nothing more for the big box store in the transaction.

They're tearing down one of the older buildings downtown. Soon, it will enter the same darkness of history which hides my great grandfather, James Stewart's, saloon. The places which once formed my familiar world are gradually disappearing from both my memory and from the physical world to make way for worlds yet to come for observers yet to be. Great grandfather Stewart died a wealthy man from the proceeds of his saloon. It was a big deal in Ashland, serving the arrivals at the 15th Street dock, but where are the memories of it now? Wiped to impotence.

That, I think, is what made me so short tempered with the young woman at the big box store. In my new guise of cranky old man, I am impotent, one to be suffered if need be, but no longer a person to be cozened or accommodated. I am made so by a world which has abandoned human relationships in favor of a spreadsheet. I cannot breathe such air.

Robert E. Lee

I'm having a tough time with the state of debate in our country. Preacher that I am, I started thinking about the Ten Commandments in Exodus 20, particularly the part that goes:

You shall not make for yourself an idol, whether in the form of anything that is in heaven above, or that is on the earth beneath, or that is in the water under the earth. You shall not bow down to them or worship them

This looks to me like two commandments:

1. Don't make an idol
2. Don't worship it.

A monument is a sort of an idol – a three dimensional representation of a multi-dimensional being of much greater complexity but with all the nasty bits removed. Robert E. Lee is a good case for examination. He was a successful and well-respected Union officer for 32 years. That's a considerable career, even by today's standards, but when Virginia voted to secede he followed his state's decision, despite an offer of a Union command thus entering into an unlawful war against his own country which would cost 600,000 American lives.

Wikipedia notes, "In 1865, Lee became president of Washington College (later Washington and Lee University) in Lexington, Virginia; in that position, he supported reconciliation between North and South. He accepted 'the extinction of slavery' provided for by the Thirteenth Amendment, but opposed racial equality for African Americans ..."

The idols we have made of Lee in Confederate uniform, with his vision fixed upon an horizon never to be do not speak of his work to reconcile the country. They speak of his commitment to a vile cause set out by Alexander H. Stephens, the Vice President of the Confederacy in 1861: "Our new government['s] foundations are laid, its cornerstone rests, upon the great truth that the negro is not equal to the white man."

The real Lee embodied characteristics few people today could embrace. He had some good qualities and some frankly villainous positions, but he has become for many in the south an icon, an idol in short. Embracing the cornerstones of the Confederacy as Alexander H. Stephens expressed them is impossible, but for many, so too is turning your back on a man who is held in such high regard by so many in the south. A middle course was found. It is not his historical actions which are being honored; it is his part in "southern heritage".

Historical facts are the cobblestones upon which we must walk if we are to retain our integrity. Historical facts, like cobblestones, are uneven and rough. Rather than navigating the uneven historical landscape, we pave over the cobblestones with a simpler narrative – Lee on Traveler leading his country, even if it is to disaster. It is patent nonsense. It is time and past time that we get over Lee and Stonewall Jackson and the rest of the leaders of a treasonous and calamitous moment in our history.

Lee's career prior to 1861 was successful. So, too, was the career of Benedict Arnold who enjoyed Washington's highest confidence. Lee's action of treason against his own country left the blood of 600,000 Americans on his hands. Arnold's betrayal of West Point comes a cropper by comparison. We do not erect statues of Benedict Arnold. We erect and defend statues of Lee because we have made of him a graven image of something much darker. It is time, and past time, that we see, with clarity, the cobblestones of historical fact, lest we be further led astray.

Black Lives

In the simplest terms:

400 years ago, white people brought black people over here, enslaved them and continued to do so for 250 years, while 10 or 15 generations of white families got to grow and flourish and make choices that could make their lives better.

And then 150 years ago white people "freed" black people from slavery. But then angry white people created laws that made it impossible for them to vote, or to own land, or to have the same rights as white people. The white people even erected monuments glorifying people who actively had fought to keep the black people enslaved and hid what they were doing by deeming it "southern pride".

Then, sixty years ago, we made it "legal" for black people to vote, and to be "free" from discrimination. Angry white people still fought to keep schools segregated, and closed off neighborhoods to white people only. They made it harder for black people to get bank loans, or get quality education or health care, or to (gasp) marry a white person. All while another 2-3 generations of white families got to grow and pass their wealth down to their children and their children's children.

And then we entered an age where we had the technology to make PUBLIC the things that were already happening in private – the beatings, the stop and frisk laws, the unequal distribution of justice, the police brutality (police began in America as slave patrols designed to catch runaway slaves).

And only now, after 400+ years and 20+ generations of a white head start, are we STARTING to truly have a dialogue about what it means to be black.

White privilege doesn't mean you haven't suffered or fought or worked hard. It doesn't mean white people are responsible for the sins of our ancestors. It doesn't mean you can't be proud of who you are. But it DOES mean that we need to acknowledge that the system our ancestors created was built FOR white people. It DOES mean that we owe it to our neighbors – of all colors – to acknowledge that and work to make our world more equitable.

BLACK LIVES MATTER!

Breonna Taylor

The police had a warrant for the wrong address. The address which they entered contained no one suspected of a crime. The Attorney General says that the police announced themselves. That is hotly disputed. As reported by the New York Times,

"On June 23, the Louisville Metro Police Department released a letter of termination that it sent to [Officer] Hankison, the officer who "blindly fired" 10 rounds into a covered patio door and a window, according to the termination letter. Chief Robert Schroeder accused Hankison of violating the Police Department's policy on the use of deadly force, saying his actions were "a shock to the conscience" that discredited the Police Department."

Additionally, it may be that the actual target of the warrant had actually already been apprehended at the time Ms. Taylor was shot six times.

The defense is that the police fired in self-defense. Blindly firing 10 rounds into an occupied dwelling with no line of sight as to who might be in the line of fire is a textbook definition of wanton conduct. Would the same defense be allowed if the officers had used a fragmentation grenade in response? The fact situation as we have it presents a jury question of wanton murder or second degree manslaughter under KRS chapter 507. Self-defense is not available as a defense to either charge. [7]

Ms. Taylor's death was clearly the result of the disproportionate use of force by a poorly trained and poorly disciplined police department which saddens and frightens me. No officers with whom I worked here would have behaved so. Yet, the Grand Jury returned only Wanton Endangerment charges against one officer for wantonly firing into an adjoining apartment. Ms. Breonna Taylor was collateral damage. This is unacceptable to me, a law

---

[7] McGinnis v. Com. 875 S.W.2d 518 (1994)

enforcement professional, and is unacceptable to those who see people of color being treated wrongly by a system insensitive to their humanity and is salt in their wounds.

I am so very saddened and frightened. I have grandchildren. What will they have?

The People Beneath the Bridge

The video of the people beneath the bridge in Texas is inescapable. Thousands of people, men, women and children, in 100 degree temperature huddled beneath a concrete bridge with little to no sanitary service, food or water. Now we have even more horrifying video of Border Patrol officers, OUR officers, on horseback, whipping the people with long reins as if they were no more than cattle. It just kills me.

I'm bothered even more by the discussion about it. Here is human misery at its rawest, portrayed in awful detail all over the TV. In response, one local official said "There is no border here!" and called for more enforcement. Another said, with indignation, that these people were here illegally and seemed to feel that resolved the issue, at least for him. Others called for them to be forced back to Mexico, though they are mainly Haitians. The Federal government is sending planes to take them back to Haiti, to a government in chaos, a country flattened by a 6.7 earthquake, the very place from which they fled.

What do you think you would do if your children cried for want of food, if you had no home in which to live, if your country's environment was so chaotic as to pose a threat to your children, yet there was a place, not too far away, which seemed an island of safety for your children. Fess up. What would you do?

If we build a border wall, if we fly them back to Haiti, if we prosecute them for violating our laws, if we drive them into Mexico will not the children still cry? The thought that I hear from so many is that these people are not "our" problem, that we are unfairly being imposed upon by the tears of their children, and that someway must be found to move them off our soil so that we can stop thinking we have some moral obligation to reduce their suffering. If they are returned to Haiti, if they are pushed into Mexico, do the children not still cry?

The questions posed by the people under the bridge are terribly difficult. I agree. We can't fix everything. No one can. My fear is that we will do what we can, even donate generously to a charity, then grant ourselves permission no longer to identify with the suffering of the world. We must focus ourselves not only to the reduction of suffering but to the cultivation of compassion for we must never stop identifying with those who suffer, even though we cannot resolve their suffering. To do so is to bring about the death of our souls.

Law and Order

"Law and order" We hear that phrase so frequently that it takes on the character of a single word, "lawandorder", a contraction of two equal components into a single concept. A moment's thought, though, will reveal the fallacy of such a conjunction. "Order" is a necessary component of group living. Without an orderly society within which to live, no one could accomplish anything. Indeed, without an orderly society, we couldn't feed ourselves. The question becomes, then, how to insure an orderly society.

One answer, the one preferred by most, is "law", a set of rules by which those governed agree to abide. No killing each other. No assaulting people. Don't take what is not your own. Take the steps necessary to prevent your contagion from being transmitted to those around you. These things make an orderly society possible.

Viewed in this way, obedience to the law is our chosen method of pursuing the goal of an orderly society, rather than an end unto itself. You don't get an award for obeying the speed limit – you get a ticket for violating it and endangering those around you. The goal is maintenance of an orderly society in which all can prosper.

I hear the argument that we are a community of laws and I even agree with it, but law in a vacuum, as an idol unto itself, is tyranny. Law must serve order, must it not?

No Seat at the Table

Take a close look at this young man. His name is Taylon Bensinger and he is 20 years old. He is charged with the murder of his girlfriend, Angel Brianna Rowe, 24. I never met the young man, so I can't speculate on the sort of person he is, but I well know the expression he holds in his mug shot. I met many young men with this identical expression in their mug shots. The dead eyes. The inexpressive mouth. The hopeless impression. The ones I sent to prison always received their sentence stoically with this expression. No sense of responsibility or even resentment evident, for why should there be? They are hopeless for they are unacquainted with hope. They are estranged for they never had a seat at life's table to begin with. They are irresponsible for they were never taught to be responsible. These are all learned behaviors. Anyone who doubts that has never raised an infant. Indeed, it is no exaggeration to say that I would describe the majority of the young people I sent to prison as "infantile" rather than "evil". That is not a popular position to hold. It is much more pleasing to characterize those with whom I dealt as "criminals", making them other than we are so I suffered a lot of push back on the point.

> "Why should I, or anybody else, care what happens to Taylon Bensinger? He killed his girlfriend! She was only 24! His actions ended a young life, one who shared affection with him. Is there anything worse? Whatever happens to him is too good for him. To hell with Taylon Bensinger and good riddance."

He's 20 years old.

> "Doesn't matter! Look at what he did and what an awful person he is! Hanging's too good for him!"

He's 20 years old, and what do you know of him or his upbringing? He got a driver's license less than four years ago and is not yet old enough to legally buy alcohol.

> "Yeah, but I bet that didn't stop him, and not just alcohol, either, I bet."

Can't argue with you there. I don't know him. Many, most even, of the people I sent to prison were druggies. I just think we should try to look a little deeper into things.

> "Deeper, schmeeper. Nobody made them take drugs!"

Maybe. Maybe.

> "They made their beds. Now they can just lie in them. It's their fault, not mine, and I don't owe anything to human trash."

Maybe. Maybe. I remember the boys on the back row of seats in elementary school. They mostly came from impoverished families and the teachers, generally, did not ask them questions for their experience had taught them well that they would receive no answers. The boys on the back row were not college-bound, so they were not interested in involving themselves in the lessons presented. They were not motivated to succeed for success was not a part of their family's culture. I saw the boys from the back row often during my career as prosecutor. They did not act responsibly for to be such would have been to leave their family, their community, which also did not understand so abstract a quality, and they had not the strength to leave their only support.

> "Oh! So what are we supposed to do, then? Just let them get away with it?"

Now you raise a profound question. Something must be done, I agree. A life has been taken. The question is precisely as you have stated it, "What are we supposed to do, then?"

> "I'll tell you what to do with them! Lock them up and throw away the key. Their kind is what is wrong with America today and it's getting worse the more we molly-coddle them."

My grandson is two years old. He has no sense of responsibility at all. If he wants something, he reaches for it and if he doesn't get it, he wails until he does. His strategy is, "I want! I will make those around me get it for me." Is my grandson to also be locked up?

> "You are out of your mind! That's what two-year-olds do! We have to expect people this fool's age to do better than that, don't we?"

Where will they learn that? Who will teach them if their families did not?

> "Hell! I don't know! Anybody with any decency in them knows these things."

And now, we've come to the crux of the matter. In the view of those arguing for harsher and harsher penalties, responsibility and decency are qualities of a righteous human being and their absence marks a man as a villain. It has never been so simple. All people share both the good and the bad qualities we recognize so easily in our brothers and sisters. Alexander Solzhenitsyn nailed it,

> **"If only it were all so simple! If only there were evil people somewhere insidiously committing evil deeds, and it were necessary only to separate them from the rest of us and destroy them. But the line dividing good and evil cuts through the heart of every human being. And who is willing to destroy a piece of his own heart?"**

There's no need to extend this further. Recognizing a duty toward those who have offended our laws to bring out the better within them is hard. Despising such people is satisfying, for it highlights our own righteousness.

> Out of the ground the Lord God made to grow every tree that is pleasant to the sight and good for food, the tree of life also in the midst of the garden, and the tree of the knowledge of good and evil. [8] ...but of the tree of the knowledge of good and evil you shall not eat, for in the day that you eat of it you shall die." [9]

---

[8] Genesis 2:9 NRSV
[9] Genesis 2:17 NRSV

Kirk Street

When I'm not under time pressure, which is the ordinary course of things at my time of life, I sometimes take Kirk Street home from church. Kirk Street connects with Stewart Avenue, which is named in my honor (it isn't but the thought amuses me). For perhaps a block and a half on Stewart Avenue I travel the forest primeval. It is exactly like the forests in which I spent my youth, far, apparently, from the strictures of adult-mandated life yet quite close enough that I should not fall into serious danger.

Stewart Avenue connects with Morgan Avenue which connects to Highland Avenue, to which I sometimes bicycled in hopes of catching a glimpse of a classmate I deemed to be the daintiest thing beneath a bonnet in all of Ashland, Kentucky. I want to be clear that I am not carrying a torch here. Mrs. Schneider has been very clear with me about such things. What I am doing is reconnecting, in some way, to a time when life was not so awful, a time when we didn't have a horrible election campaign, when we didn't have to consider two hurricanes and an asteroid strike on top of a pandemic. A time, in short, when life was more manageable.

In a short time, I will die. Not next Tuesday, perhaps. Perhaps not for many years, but I'm 74 years of age. I do not anticipate living to the ripe old age of 148, so, relatively speaking, in a short time, I'll die. That colors the way I see our country, because it often appears to me to be as moribund as am I. We were founded on concepts so optimistic, yet have turned out, or so it seems to me, so differently. One third of our people think a man who jokes "Twelve more years" is a good person to have about. Many of our people hear this man say "Cut down on the testing and the virus will go away. It will be like a miracle." and believe him. What has happened to us that we so easily and thoughtlessly cast away the responsibilities we granted ourselves at such great cost?

In the forest of Stewart Avenue I can set aside these thoughts and pretend myself to be a child again, but the noise of the disassembly of my beloved nation lurks around the curve, clambering for attention. One of my fellow Americans even asserted today, without a hint of awareness of her heresy, that unless we vote for this man, our country will lose its status as a God-beloved nation.

Take me back to the forest primeval. I am in such fear!

Chad Mitchell

Yesterday, Chad Mitchell came up on my player singing "The Strangest Dream". Those of you as well decayed as am I may remember the lyrics

Last night I had the strangest dream

I never had before.

I dreamed the world had all agreed

To put an end to war.

The lyrics interrupted my thoughts about the COVID pandemic and the resistance to mask wearing. Before I was aware of what was happening, two opposing trains of thought pulled up chairs at the table in my mind and began discussing the matter.

Chad Mitchell: There can be no question that war is an appalling waste of time, lives and resources and that there is no reasonable defense to it!

Unmasked man: That's bull! If we don't defend our rights, we'll lose them. Any fool can see that you can't let people push you around. You have to resist! There is no more closely held right than that of self-defense.

Chad Mitchell: Oh yes there is, too. The care we owe to others not to harm them is a more important consideration, and you know it. You're just too afraid!

Unmasked man: I'll show you something to be afraid of! I love this land (waves a flag) and there is no sacrifice I would not make to protect her.

Chad Mitchell: Then why won't you wear a mask to protect your fellow Americans from this virus? That's a pretty small sacrifice, seems to me.

Unmasked man: Apples and oranges! What I love about America is that at least I know I'm free! I'm free to make my own decisions about what I'll do and if you try to take my liberty away, you're in for a hell of a fight.

Chad Mitchell: I guess that's what I'm thinking about. There is a simple thing we could do to slow the spread of this virus, but what if someone, such as you, refuses to cooperate? How do we enforce it? You immediately jump to something akin to war. It's like I just sang, if the world had all agreed to put an end to war, how would you enforce it, for you know there are those who would try to turn that decision to their own profit.

Unmasked man: I don't know anything about profit. What I'm talking about is my God-given right to make decisions about what I will do and I've got a basement full of guns that says nobody's going to take that right away.

Chad Mitchell: So…if I understand you…war or some sort of armed conflict is the only way to assure peace and cooperation? You're telling me that without a credible show of ability to inflict death there can be no life?

Me: My stomach hurts…

Hard Work

I was leaving an Ashland retail store (OK...the liquor store) and pulled into the alley. My attention was drawn to the brick pavement. Brick pavement isn't unusual in Ashland. Ashland's streets were paved with hand-laid brick, even the alleys. Many men on their knees, foot by foot, mile by mile, laid down brick pavers to make the roads passable in any weather.

I once said to an older friend, "I can't imagine how disheartening that must have been to look at endless stretches of dirt road, and to realize the time it would take to pave them, foot by foot, mile by mile."

"That's not what they were thinking", he corrected me. "They were thinking how many paychecks there would be to get to the end of that road."

That was the America, largely mythical, which we reference in our imaginations – hard work leading to independence – but that is assuredly not the America in which we now live. Young people today, if they can find work at all, are paid less than a living wage. We are telling our children, "If you work hard and apply yourself, you get nothing."

That cannot be the bequest we leave our children. We cannot continue to devalue honest labor without risking tragedy and we owe it to our children to do better.

Gone With the Wind

My poor memory is so damaged I couldn't say if I ever saw "Gone With the Wind" or not. With the controversy over the film, Kathy and I watched the first 2 hours last night. Viewed with 2020 sensibilities, I observed a few things:

1. It is preceded by a disclaimer about the depictions of race as it should be. That's responsible.

2. That said, I couldn't help but notice that in the first 2 hours at least, it is the characters of color who are behaving like adults while the white characters are cheering the onset of a war which would take more American lives than all subsequent wars combined. It is the white women who are behaving like spoiled adolescents. Scarlet's childishness is most clearly mirrored by Prissy, who can be forgiven for she IS a child.

3. Most tellingly though, I watched Scarlet's selfish insistence on returning to Tara, to the old way of life, rather than toward repentance and healing.

I understand the disclaimer. I understand the evil of racial stereotyping (though I think Song of the South is worse), but I think that people of color can see much in the black characters in which to be proud. They were the grownups. And of course, there's the wonderful Hattie McDaniel.

The Fairness Doctrine

CNN just presented a piece on changes at Fox and I began thinking about the "Fairness Doctrine". As explained by Wikipedia, "The fairness doctrine of the United States Federal Communications Commission (FCC), introduced in 1949, was a policy that required the holders of broadcast licenses to both present controversial issues of public importance and to do so in a manner that was honest, equitable, and balanced. The FCC eliminated the policy in 1987 and removed the rule that implemented the policy from the Federal Register in August 2011. The fairness doctrine had two basic elements: It required broadcasters to devote some of their airtime to discussing controversial matters of public interest, and to air contrasting views regarding those matters."

This struck me because of a conversation I had yesterday on Facebook with a long-time colleague and classmate. My friend has a long history of civil interactions with me and others and he is a man for whom I have great respect. Yesterday, to my consternation, he jumped into a discussion of President Obama with an assertion that the Obama administration was scandal-ridden. Several people, including me, expressed puzzlement and others demanded that he explain himself. This was his explanation:

> **"Oh let's see what you are too stupid to know. IRS, Veterans deaths, Benghazi, fast and furious, Biden and his idiot son, social security and Lois Lerner, the Impeachment farce that Obama and Biden knew was bullshit and aided the conspiracy by their silence, Obama Care and you can keep your Doctor and each family will save $2,000 knowing it was a lie, DOJ, FBI and FISA warrants. Just for starters! Obviously neither you or whoever Bruce is can't read or refuse to. Stick it where the light don't shine boys!!"**

That was so spectacularly unlike my colleague that I immediately suspected he was ill or that we were speaking to an impostor. I responded with, "If you are really the man I know and respect, you don't sound like you. Are you Ill?"

This kicked off another slew of condescending, imprecise, rude and self-aggrandizing responses from him, stating clearly that those who disagreed with him were either stupid or ill.

What struck me so strongly was the list he provided. They are not "scandals", they are watch-words, key phrases known by a community but obscure to those not within the community. These are the flags around which his community gather jointly to celebrate their strength. I can't begin to say how badly this hurt. This is a man I have known half a century, a man I respect, a man who can engage in civil discourse, become now toxic and partisan.

How could this happen?

I withdrew from the conversation and retired to my office to think about what had happened. My mind naturally turned to Fox as I had heard some of those phrases from other Fox viewers. I turned on Fox to sample what was being said.

To my surprise, I lasted less than a minute. Thanks to the abandonment of the Fairness Doctrine, their broadcasts are founded upon a collection of shared assumptions which are beyond question. This shared assumption set permits Fox viewers to reason themselves to the conclusions my friend expressed. The weakness is, of course, that if the assumptions are false, the conclusions must fall as well. Take, for example, the assertion that the 2020 election was stolen. From that foundational assumption you can easily conclude the existence of a deep state conspiracy large enough to accomplish such a task. The objection that there is no evidence of voter fraud sufficient to change the outcome is powerless to counter the argument for to accept that statement is to counter the foundational assumption set, the very shibboleth of the community's unity.

I mourn the loss of my colleague, with whom I can no longer speak without sacrificing my integrity. I mourn for my country who has become mesmerized by forces little in their ken. I mourn.

Face Masks

Reason teaches me that when faced by a disease which has already claimed 681,000 American lives, something both as effective and as trivial as a face mask would not come to be the center of controversy it has become. But it has.

I also learned this week that my former father-in-law died. I wish I could generate some appropriate emotion about that, but I cannot. Lee would have been on the side of never wearing a mask. He was stubbornly uninformed and I cannot keep myself from suspecting that something of the same is fueling the antimaskers.

When I say that Lee was uninformed, I don't mean that he was learning disabled. He lived a long life, and supported himself and his families, but Lee knew little about the world, and much preferred it to be that way. What he had learned of the world as a child in Portsmouth, Ohio (pronounced "Porchmuff") was all he wished to know of it. He stubbornly refused to engage any new or contradictory information about the world and its workings. Lee would not have worn a mask. To do so would be to admit that there is more to the world than his preferred, limited, view and he defended that view fiercely. Within that world, he was safe. Even the smallest excursion from it frightened him.

And so we have a virus stalking the land, and to understand the threat, one must understand things such as the size of virus particles, arcane topics like "messenger RNA", droplets, epidemiology, and other exotica which would only emphasize to one like Lee how little he knew. Worse yet, once engaged, such knowledge would lead him not to a less stressful life, but to one which would frighten him. Lee would not have engaged the debate. He would have done as we see many doing, turned on his heel and embraced the less threatening view of life given him as a child in Porchmuff.

These, as I see them, are the parameters of the debate. On the one side are those with actual training, who are saying that this virus will kill us unless we pull together. On the other side are people (tragically lead by the President) saying loudly, "You're not the boss of me. It will just go away. It will be like a miracle." What they are really saying, I believe, is, "My self-respect, my sense of self-worth, rests upon my ignorance being granted worth and value as great as your knowledge." The only ones who will do so are those like them, the stubbornly uninformed. So are we split.

I mourn for our people.

The Dunning-Kruger Effect

The Dunning-Kruger effect is, "a cognitive bias in which people of low ability have illusory superiority and mistakenly assess their cognitive ability as greater than it is. The cognitive bias of illusory superiority comes from the inability of low-ability people to recognize their lack of ability. Without the self-awareness of metacognition, low-ability people cannot objectively evaluate their competence or incompetence."

When I first learned of the Dunning-Kruger effect, it immediately "clicked" with me because it states so precisely that no man knows that which he does not know. If I know nothing about carpentry (and I don't), I am simply unaware of the nuances and complexities of the art, but am likely to think that all there is to carpentry is hammering nails and cutting wood, and what's so hard about that? I got my comeuppance in seventh grade Industrial Arts, along with a lot of wasted wood and some blood.

I've already confessed to being a confused and often arrogant old man, so it's not surprising that I mentally shortened that definition of the Dunning-Kruger effect to something like, "Dumb people just are not smart enough to know they should listen to their betters", then, Appalachian native that I am, I softened that harsh assessment by adding, "Bless their hearts".

Lately, though, as I prowl through the basements of my mind, I began to think again of Dunning-Kruger and the President of the United States. Let me say, right up front, that I am not a fan. The man is appallingly uninformed. He appears to have the attention span of a fruit fly. His full attention is applied only to actions which make him look powerful and he has a nasty streak of authoritarianism that scares me witless. This assessment is so self-evident that I am at a loss to understand even his weak popularity. How are we to understand the fierce loyalty shown by so many to this dangerous and ignorant man?

Of course, I immediately turned to Messrs. Dunning and Kruger for an explanation. Mr. Trump, a person of low cognitive ability, grants validation to other low-ability people to continue in their comfortable ways without examining any other courses. There. That must explain it.

Except, it doesn't, or at the very least, doesn't completely explain it. Travel with me to visit my great-grandfather, Johannes Nicholas Schneider, born 24 Jun 1845 in Kaisersesch, Rheinland-Pfalz, Germany. He arrived in this country in 1872, a young man of 27 who, I presume, spoke little or no English. What a cacophony America must have been! Impenetrable language, baffling customs, strange people. Had I been him, I would have curled into a self-protective bubble and that is exactly what he did. He traveled half-way across the country to Calumet, Wisconsin and settled there, among German people with largely German customs. Most importantly, Calumet was a place where German was spoken. His son, my grandfather, didn't learn English until high school.

It is only because of my cognitive bias of intellectual superiority that I can make such harsh judgments of Trump supporters for I have not walked in the shoes of those for whom the demands of 21st Century living is just the sort of a cacophony which met Nicholas on his arrival in New York. I cannot experience the relief felt by those for whom living is a confusion when the President tells them that the world is not complicated. The virus will be defeated in no time. Fifteen cases and soon it will be zero. Climate change is unimportant. Soon it will be cooler. China is the enemy, and just like you who toil at dead-end and low paid jobs, whose lives are controlled by forces beyond your ken, the United States is being treated unfairly by these other, foreign, countries.

It is to that sense of victim-hood and bafflement that Trump hitches his political aspirations, and it is powerful medicine as even a cursory look at pre-World War II history will demonstrate. The challenge faced by this country is existential and it must be taken up if we wish to survive. We are challenged to acknowledge that no man, not even educated ones, know that which they do not know. We are challenged to understand the forces which drive the Trump machine as more than simple ignorance, but as a deep cry of distress by those within our country who have, too often, been written off. Should we fail to engage this challenge fully, I fear for the future of my children.

Dreams

I am fascinated by dreams, the more so as age robs me of my memories. Life runs through me, carving the profiles of my coastline but when the tide has receded, often all that remains is those coastlines which my mind offers back to me not as memories but as distillations in the form of dreams.

At my age, many of those dreams reflect my distress as I navigate a world in which I often find myself confused and disoriented. In one I recall, I'm in an alley in Catlettsburg. Nothing looks familiar except the flood wall to my right. To my left are the back portions of businesses, mostly the worse for wear. I am searching for the way back to familiar territory, but every turn leads me to more unfamiliar streets, always with the flood wall beside me.

In another, my cousin, Dennis, walked me through a strange western town, a portion of which was on fire. He assured me that was normal for that part of town. On the distant edge of town, he bid me farewell and told me to have fun with the park. Poof! Once again, I was alone and lost with nothing but the flaming downtown to guide me. Oh, and a river, complete with a flood wall.

One of the most telling found me driving a mature woman (perhaps a teacher?) along Winchester Avenue near the old Coke plant. I was interested in what she was saying and when I returned my attention to the road, we were in an industrial area completely unknown to me. I apologized and tried to find my way back to Terra cognito, but the roads became ever more confusing. Now I was in an elderly village of sorts with many tiny shops and older businesses. I left my car to inquire for directions, leaving the woman in the car. No one could tell me anything beyond that I was in Westwood, nor how to get back to Ashland.

This is where the trumpet sounded for me. As I was asking yet another man for directions he was unable to give, it occurred to me that I must be dreaming. That was it! None of this was real. All I had to do was to wake up! But … how do you do that if what is before your eyes is so indisputably real? What do you do with a foreign world to force it back into your lifetime expectations?

I don't want to jinx myself, but overall I do pretty well with my vascular dementia. My two biggest stumbling blocks are recall and spacial amnesia. If Kathy tells me to go to Walmart, she has to tell me how to get there. The next time, she must tell me again. Mostly, if I'm alone, I drive until I see something familiar. Not always, but often. I'm not alone in this. I remember hearing a silver alert for a colleague of many years past, a man who spent as many years in the courts as did I but who is much deeper in the swamp than am I. He wandered off and became lost. Are these dreams revealing my fears for the future? Almost certainly. How do you wake up, if what is before your eyes appears real? How does knowing you are in a dream lessen the suffering of being lost?

Farrell

My second cousin's name was Farrell. He suffered from uncontrollable epilepsy and lived in a small brown room at the back of his mother's house. There was little hope for epileptics in those days, and he never held a job. Twice a week he walked a block and a half to the Bluegrass Grill and bought a strawberry pie. Other than that, he seldom left the house.

When I was young, I saw Farrell only once a year. On Christmas day, we would all pile into the Plymouth and drive to his mother's house to give them a fruitcake. Farrell would come out of his room and try, embarrassingly hard, to make polite conversation with us. More often than not, he would wind up telling enormously long stories. They must have seemed witty to him, since he guffawed a lot as he told them, but I could barely follow what he was saying and my mind would wander. At a certain point, I would begin watching the door, praying that we would get out of there soon. Finally, my father would clap both hands on his knees and stand up saying, "Well, we've got many more stops tonight. Merry Christmas!" and then, in a rush of coats and hats and long woolen scarves collected from the horsehair sofa in the front room, we would be gone for another year.

As I grew older, I paid less and less attention to Farrell's stories. They washed right over me, with no more effect than the blare of the television his mother kept running the whole length of our visit. Farrell's voice became just one more noise to be endured until that blessed clap on the knees that signaled my salvation for another year.

Eventually the visits stopped. I went to college, graduated and came back, but there didn't seem to be the same need to deliver fruitcakes anymore. Without the visit, Farrell disappeared from my world. He was a childhood memory for me now rather than a living human being.

It therefore came as a great surprise when I was startled awake one night from a terrifying nightmare. In the dream, Farrell was standing across a wide street from me. With an exaggerated motion of his arm, he was beckoning me to cross the four lanes of traffic that separated us. His expression was utterly blank, but I knew that he wanted to tell me something of great importance. Again and again, I stepped into the road to try to reach him. Each time, however, the traffic picked up. Horns blared, and trucks and cars and great yellow buses hurtled between us. My path was blocked and I couldn't get to him. I woke with a start. The next morning, my father called to tell me that Farrell had unexpectedly died that night.

I think I can come to terms with the idea that something of Farrell reached out to me at the moment of his death. But why couldn't I cross the road? I'd like to think that there is a chasm between the living and the dead, a gulf that mortal flesh cannot cross, not even in sleep. Perhaps that is why I was prevented from hearing that last story he wanted to tell me. But it may be that on those endless visits, so long ago, I learned too well how to ignore another human being, a man living out his life in a brown room at the back of his mother's house.

Wampus

There was a character in my youth who I called "Uncle Morton". When not meddling in local politics, he was treasurer of Ashland Sanitary Milk Company, the dairy founded by my grandfather. Uncle Morton was, properly speaking, my second cousin, not my uncle, and he was better known in the community by his nickname, "Wampus Montgomery".

One summer, I was hired by my dad to count the coins from the milk machines he maintained at Armco. Lots and lots of coins, big bags of coins, so many that there were two machines which sorted, counted and rolled them for deposit. My job was to pour the coins into the hopper to be counted and then to hold the coin wrappers as the other machine efficiently filled them. It was not challenging work.

Until it was. I came up 25¢ short.

Yes, children, there was a time in my lifetime when 25¢ actually held purchasing power. I set about trying to find that quarter for the full afternoon, with no success. As the day waned, Uncle Morton came into my counting house and demanded to know why he did not have stacks of wrapped coins to take to the bank.

I sheepishly told him of the missing quarter and, in desperate hope of putting the thing behind me, offered to deposit a quarter of my own.

"You will not!" he roared. "That is not a quarter. That is a clear flag that there is something wrong with the accounts and you will sit there until the accounts are reconciled."

As an adult I can see just how right Wampus was. Two columns of figures representing different perspectives on the same event which fail to agree is a clear flag that there is something wrong. That is the adult view. I was not an adult. To me, it appeared that all could be made well again for a trifling amount of money, so why wouldn't you? A child focuses on the small things. That is a child's perspective. An adult must be aware of the bigger picture. This is an adult's perspective. The child's perspective puts stress away quickly and painlessly. The adult's perspective engages the problem in an effort to restore wholeness to the system.

As it turned out, the quarter was (ahem) hiding under the machine and I eventually got to go home, a wiser and more adult young man but I have carried Wampus with me ever since. This is by way of explaining why I have spent the entire weekend trying to find $19.30 which represents the out of balance state of my banking this month, all the while hearing Wampus roaring in the background, and why tonight I expect I will not sleep at all, due to the entry marked "Fudge" in my Miscellaneous column.

Die Krankenhaus

As this dream opened, I was a patient in a nursing home for the critically ill. I knew I was a patient for I was dressed in a hospital gown which I wore like a robe. I was ambulatory and felt called, compelled really, to visit with the other patients to offer comfort and a listening ear. In the dream, I was quite comfortable in that role, but in the morning, I found it terribly difficult to write about. It embarrassed me to have seen myself in a Jesus-like role, robe and all. I confessed to my discomfort on Facebook. Almost immediately came a reply from a Facebook friend:

> I found it interesting that you felt so uncomfortable in the role of helping others, as if you were presumptuously impersonating Jesus when Jesus himself directed his followers to do just that - take care of their fellow humans. Being perfect was never a requisite.

> While it is true we are flawed, the imperative and emphasis of organized theology that we must constantly apologize and 'atone' for being human is, I think emotionally/psychologically damaging. Imagine if every day you constantly recited your child's flaws to him and reminded him he'd never be 'good enough' to earn your love but that because you're such a benevolent parent, you'll acknowledge him as yours and allow him to inherit IF he (fill in the blank) according to the theology)

> It seems we as humans constantly strive to BE ENOUGH.

> I'm constantly trying to figure out the whats and whys of this life, but often wonder what it would be like to just BE rather than constantly STRIVE TO BE.

It's easy to see why I preview these musings on Facebook – this stopped me in my tracks. In the dream, my character had become a sort of an island of peace for people in the home and I felt uncomfortable writing about that. Why would that be? What oddly carved coastal landscape of my past was being offered to me? What contemporary issues might have called forth such a reaction?

In the dream, my activities were ignored by the administration of the nursing home as I was causing it no particular difficulty and, anyway, so long as my activities were limited to offering comfort, it was benefiting the administration as well because it cut down on complaints.

Eventually, however, the medical staff of the administration determined that my "breathing difficulty" might be improved if I were bound in a prone position, face down, on a table. Perhaps I had crossed a line somewhere? Once I was bound, the dream shifted from a first person account to a narrative. The narrator reported that the treatment, far from improving my condition, caused serious breathing difficulty for the patient who desperately attempting to raise himself up on hands and knees, painfully gasping for breath.

At this point, something happened which wasn't clear, but the administration disappeared and the patients took on themselves the duties of the administration, including the care of the patients. There was a general feeling of elation as they moved into this new role, a celebration of what they believed was a liberation and a grant of independence from the unpleasant and sometimes painful treatments imposed by the previous administration. They spoke of "personal choice".

Some of the patients, natural charismatics, took on leadership roles and responsibility for patient care plans. The leading value was "maximized happiness" and decisions were made to assure that the community itself could enjoy maximum happiness. There was general rejoicing by all who were, of course, exhausted by their earlier lives under the previous administration – lives of regimented doses of medicine and therapy for their own good which only served to focus their attention upon their mortality and eventual death. It was exhausting. The new people's administration, however, offered to take that burden from them and impose happiness for all. It was greeted with almost hysterical celebration.

Of course, life being life, there were some in the community who were moribund and others who could not embrace the community celebration, and these members were a stain on the overall celebratory air. Something must be done with such people, lest the buzz be harshed. Eventually, it was determined that, since they were going to die in any event it would be an act of unkindness to extend their misery, really a sin against happiness, and so a policy of discontinuing medication to ease their passage from their personal veil of tears was adopted. After a time, the patient/leaders became convinced that since many took too long in their suffering to die even after being deprived of their medicine, leaving their deaths to chance was not a kindness to the community. After careful examination of medical records, if death was believed to be inevitable, it would be a contribution of kindness to the community to ease them out painlessly. A policy of euthanasia was adopted.

The main character (no longer me), not deemed sick enough to die, was released from his restraints and allowed again to roam the campus. Now, however, he brought a message not of comfort and peace but one of condemnation. He confronted the patient committee members wherever he encountered them with harsh looks of condemnation, telling them that they had no rights to the powers they had assumed. He was sternly warned that he had no authority to stand in judgment of the patient committee, who were acting solely in the interest of maximum happiness.

After I posted my dream on Facebook, another friend replied, "Awesome dream. Kinda neat that there are these different people in you!"

Oh my heavenly days! He's right!

Powerlessness

In this dream, I was again an Assistant Commonwealth's Attorney. I came into the office to find that someone had altered all the computers – the system I had designed. In place of a screen, each now had a typewriter like device on them so that all output was on paper. Worse yet, the system I had so diligently designed and written had been replaced by something new which made no sense at all and produced no usable output. The Commonwealth's Attorney couldn't have cared less. He didn't use or understand the computer system and didn't wish to. I was on my own. He brushed me off. I was furious and began thrashing about, waking Kathy. She woke me and we returned to sleep. I returned to the same dream.

In the second take on the dream, I was now in charge. I asked who had done this thing and was told by our secretary, that "the nasty woman from downstairs came and did this". I howled that this was unacceptable and she agreed, but could offer no solution. I ran down the stairs to find the "nasty woman".

She was young, attractive, and utterly contemptuous of my fury. All she had done, she said, was to correct an inefficient system (the one of my design) with a modern and better system. She really couldn't grasp why I should be angry. I went to her supervisor and was told much the same. When I screamed that she had erased 13 years of filing, he shrugged and assured me that she had backed it up, somewhere. "WHERE?", I screamed back. He shrugged. The world had changed. I wished it to be returned to as it was. I ordered the woman to my office to repair the damage. She came with me. It was clear that she was not taking me seriously, but only accompanying me for lack of anything better to do. That infuriated me further still.

Now the typewriter output devices had sprouted antennae. "What is THAT?" I shouted. "That's the more modern way to do output", she replied with emphasized calmness. This is when I ripped the typewriter devices off. As it turned out, I was ripping the covers off Kathy. She woke me and I came downstairs.

What threads are being pulled in this dream, as it relates to a person who has never been this old before and isn't all that pleased with the situation in which he finds himself? First, there is the thread of vulnerability. At my age, I am vulnerable, both to the actions of others, malicious or not, and to the forces of change. I complained to my doctor the other day of urinary frequency. I told her that she had me on a diuretic but that I enjoyed drinking iced tea, which also has a diuretic property. I wondered if I could forego the pill. "No", she instructed me. "Stop drinking tea." She had my best interest in mind. She wasn't being malicious. She just thought it in my best interest to remove from my life one more thing that gives me pleasure. As her patient, I am vulnerable to her instructions.

The second thread that occurs to me is that of impotence. There was a time when I could cause things to happen by a simple order. That time is past. No one need heed me now, except from impulses of kindness. The woman who had damaged my computers went with me as I directed not from any misapprehension of my power to compel her to do so, but from her estimate that to do so was the best way to get the old man to calm down.

These are the threads which lifted me from a dream to thrash in my bed with such violence that I struck Kathy. These are the threads which bind me to a bed of torment over my changed existence. I mourn for my lost power and self-actuation. I fear my vulnerability to something unexpected like a fall or an illness. I see my classmates and old friends depart and am aware of my powerlessness to hold back the hands of time.

This is the bitter soup of old age. Some fool counseled a rape victim once, saying that if it is going to happen just relax and enjoy it. FOOL! Listen to Dylan Thomas:

Do not go gentle into that good night,
Old age should burn and rave at close of day;
Rage, rage at the dying of the light.

Death and Violence

From my position here on the couch it seems clear that the universe is lining up things for me to think about, just to see what it does to me. Three things got lined up for me this time.

First, my mother-in-law is recuperating with us. That brings her preferences for television into our home. Mom is very fond of westerns. I haven't watched a western since Shep was a pup, and had not thought about them in longer than that, for there is little to think about in a western. Basically, bad guys do bad things for no clearly examined reasons and are stopped by a good guy who shoots them with no consequences. The body is left on the street for some less interesting character to clean up, while the good guys retire to the saloon for a well-earned drink. Even as a child I wondered about the guy who had to pick up the bodies. Were bad guys given funerals?

Secondly, for the past 12 days I have been shown video of Hamas rockets and Israeli rockets pounding down buildings in the other's territory. Honestly, it looks to me an awful lot like Matt Dillon facing off against the bad guy in front of Miss Kitty's saloon. I can't help wondering what is the point in killing children of the other side. That's going to make things better?

Finally, just before I came in here to write, there was a commercial for a gun show, called "Fire Power" on the TV. I was urged to "come on down" and "stock up on guns and ammo". Stock up? What is up with the veneration of violence? Our fathers fought pure evil, in the person of the Nazis, in the only way they knew how – death and violence. They were successful in destroying, for a time, the Nazi scourge. Then they came home and played out their experiences on the television and movie screens, translated onto a canvas of the 19th Century West. Their children, my generation, watched as well, and learned the lesson of the good guys and the bad guys. Bad guys are born that way. Good guys must use the tools and skills learned in World War II to exterminate the bad guys lest our country be overrun.

Perhaps it is the intensity of repetition which has given the good guys/bad guys meme such fertile root in my mind. Perhaps that is behind some of the odd dreams I have. Like this one.

My antagonist last night was Pure Evil, as represented by a middle-aged white male. I don't know what he was threatening to do which allowed me to identify him as Pure Evil, but that's neither here nor there. I was armed with a double-barreled 12 gauge, and was directing him not to do whatever he had threatened. I remember clearly placing the barrels beneath his chin.

He looked at me with disdain as if both of us knew how unlikely it would be that I would successfully carry through with such a threat. What struck me was his attitude that whatever followed was on me, not on him. Pure Evil can be that way, I've found.

The impasse was too great. I pulled the front trigger. Click! I pulled the back trigger. Click. No explosion. The look of satisfaction on the face of Pure Evil was almost more than I could bear. I retrieved the shotgun from beneath his chin and reloaded, replacing it. Now the trigger guard had gone and the triggers were, well, flaccid. I couldn't even manage a Click! The look of derision on the face of Pure Evil had now become one of amusement and almost pity. He had me! I had tried to blow his head off, and I had failed.

What followed was a succession of attempts, with different firearms, to kill Pure Evil. I even recruited neighbors to assist, holding Pure Evil so that he could not wiggle away and dodge the bullets. Each time, he fell to the ground, appearing to be mortally wounded, only to rise again. In desperation, I grabbed a flare gun and aimed squarely at his chest. The flare hit, and fire spit from his face, his mouth and eyes, a demonic display. Surely, I had him now!

He rose again in triumph and laughed at me.

I woke, feeling ill, and went to the bathroom. I was ashamed of my dream, both that I had failed, but more so because I had tried to destroy evil by evil's own means.

Beyond demonstrating that I am insufferably didactic, even asleep, I can't help but feel there was something significant about these dreams. I'll think on them.

Cousin's Passing

I met my remaining first cousin, Dennis, in the Grand Junction, Colorado airport this week. I had not seen him in 63 years. How is that even possible? How can I have a conversation with a man about things which happened 63 years ago and more?

The occasion which brought us together after so many years was the death of his sister, Gail, who was my only other first cousin. Kathy and I were there to join in a celebration of Gail's life, arranged by her husband, Rob. Denny and Gail's father is long dead. Their mother lived to 101 but is now gone. My mother and father are dead, as is my brother, Jimmy, and even my son, Johnny. Dennis and I have outlived our family, and only we two are there to remember their time in Ashland.

They lived in my grandfather Stewart's house. It was situated on the top of Prospect hill, and was believed to be the second brick house built in Pogue's Landing, the settlement which became Ashland. The family story was that the bricks from which it was built had been made on site. The builders came first to clear the land, second to build a brick kiln, then to bake the bricks, stacking them on pallets, and only then to build the house. My mom's brother, Jimmy, his wife "Aunt Percy" and their two children lived in an apartment on the second floor. The mysteries of that old house, 102 years old then, were our shared experience. Particularly the basement, for the house had been built directly on the ground, and the basement excavated in interlocking tunnels filled with mystery for any child brave enough to explore them. These would be the memories Dennis and I would have to excavate to find any shared memories 63 years later.

Oddly, we recognized ourselves immediately in the airport though time and trouble had changed us so. We shook hands awkwardly, uncertain of how much intimacy was appropriate in this meeting between two strangers. As time went on, we relaxed a bit, until it was time for the Celebration of Gail's life.

Gail had taught public school for 30 years. The venue, a vineyard, was filled to overflowing with her colleagues and friends, for there was little family left. Dennis has a lovely daughter and she had a very nice husband. Gail had a daughter of some note in her field and her husband. I had family I had forgotten and family I did not know.

When the time came, friends and family were invited to celebrate their time with Gail. Dennis tried powerfully, but could not. Neither could Rob. I stood up to give my memories of Gail, but she left when she was six or seven. I realized that although we spent every Tuesday with them (while mom played golf) Dennis and I were two years older, an immense gulf at that age, so we became "the big uns" and Gail and Jimmy "the little uns". My memories were of things the big uns did. We paid little attention to what Gail and Jimmy did to entertain themselves.

I had only one memory to relate — the day Uncle Jimmy and his family left for Youngstown, Ohio. Of course, Denny and I had no way to relate to what was happening. The thought that we might be separated for 63 years was simply not possible to entertain. But I did still have a memory of the day they left. We were in Granddad's kitchen. The adults said their goodbyes while we children looked on unknowing, then, with a final goodbye, they headed for the door, Uncle Jimmy in the lead, already looking forward to a new job and a new life. Aunt Percy was second, following her husband into the new life he had chosen for them. Next was Dennis, as blank about the enormity of what was happening as was I. Last came little Gail, and it was only she who seemed to grasp what was happening for as her family went through that old screen door, she turned to look at us, flashed a little girl smile, raised her little hand and said, "Bye-bye" to the family she would never see again.

Oh my heart hurts.

A Button

A most idle thought...

Kathy and her mom are watching Spencer Tracey and Katherine Hepburn in "Desk Set". The plot revolves around whether or not the "research department" where Hepburn works could be replaced by an "electronic brain" as had already happened in payroll. There was considerable anxiety about this prospect, though Hepburn insisted that no electronic brain could ever replace her department.

I thought of the woman who ran the elevators at Parson's. Her name, I think, was Suzy. She was very sweet, but her job was replaced long ago, not with an "electronic brain" but with a button. A button may be the new valuation of a human life.

That triggered speculation on people who have been replaced by buttons. When I call for an appointment, I get a computer voice asking me to push 1 for an appointment, 2 for billing, 3 for a weather report, on and on ad infinitum. Once a selection is made, my experience teaches, there will be more buttons. A transaction which could be handled in minutes between two people is stretched out for no reason other than to save the corporation the expense of hiring human operators. This does not fill me with admiration for the wise folk in IT. It fills me with concern for the humans who are unemployed. Where does one go for employment if running the elevator at Parson's was a good fit for your abilities?

That's when a more horrifying thought crossed my mind: Once there was homo habilis. Now, there is not, for homo habilis evolved into a more competent sort of being – us. Are we now witnessing the evolution of computo buttonis – a new species which feeds on profits and view us as a farmer might view his field – useful but in no way the object of true affection?

I miss telling Suzy "Fifth floor please!" and I miss her announcement of "Fifth floor. Toys and games" even more. It was a human exchange. It had nothing whatever to do with buttons.

Lost Control

My ears have begun to prick up over the phrase we hear so often in the news to describe an automobile collision. "The driver", the news person will say without the least bit of curiosity, "lost control of his vehicle", followed by some horrifying description of what might happen should you lose control of your vehicle.

"Lost control" sounds like something that happens to a driver, not something the driver did. It sounds as if the driver was diligently operating the controls when, with no warning, the steering wheel came off in his hands and he lost control of the vehicle. Well, of course he did. He's sitting there with the steering wheel in his lap.

I think we're being led up a holler here. What actually happened, I suspect, is that the vehicle was in the control of the driver, but the driver allowed his attention to be distracted. He was fooling with a phone, or trying to pick up loose change from the floor. The driver didn't lose control; he forgot to maintain it.

I'm old. Old people get grumpy over stuff like this.

The Chapel of America

Something has happened to me. I saw it coming all week, but did not give it the attention it deserved. On Sunday, it hit me like a train and I wept through my sermon. I don't know whether a part of me died, or a part was reborn.

Remember, I spent 30 years in law enforcement, as a cop and as a prosecutor. I think I have witnessed every nasty thing people do to one another. It was part of my job, and I did my job well. If it involved stepping over a body, that's what I did. I just hated the things we do to each other, the blindness we have for the humanity of others, but that was the extent of my emotional response.

Then, in Orange County, California, a mother was driving her six-year-old son to kindergarten. Aiden Leos was strapped into his booster seat when a shot was fired from another car, striking Aiden. When the bullet struck Aiden, he cried out to his Mommy, "My tummy hurts!" because that's what you do when your tummy hurts. You tell Mommy and she makes it better, but she could not. She could only hold her precious child as he died.

It just happened again. Trying to write about this has reduced this veteran prosecutor to tears again, just as it did Sunday when I tried to deliver my sermon. This just can't be. I've seen it all. I've watched bodies loaded onto ambulances. I've listened to people's excuses for the evil they have done. I'm no newby. What is the hold this little boy has on my emotions? Why can I not stop weeping? He was so young he had no way to imagine the pure evil which had struck him. All he knew was that his tummy hurt and when your tummy hurts, you tell your mommy and she makes it better, except Mommy can't make this better. It is a foulness in the very soul of a country so ill that it cannot bring itself to face its own illness.

Then, today I read that a series of mass shootings over the weekend left at least 11 people dead and another 69 injured. There were at least 12 mass shootings between Friday night and Sunday, according to CNN reporting and an analysis of data from the Gun Violence Archive (GVA), local media and police reports.

Walk with me into a very old chapel. In the dimness inside, to our left, is the statue of Jesus known as "Christ the Redeemer" from Brazil. Christ's hands are outstretched in blessing to all the people of the world. Before Him is a kneeler and an altar.

On the other side of the chapel is a statue of a white man wearing a tee shirt which says, "Militia". He is armed with two handguns, a knife and an assault rifle with an extended magazine. Before him is also a kneeler and a small altar. We are in the chapel of America.

It is plain that if you kneel before Christ the Redeemer, you must turn your back on the armed man. If you kneel before the man who revels in his personal power, you must turn your back on Christ. No, there is no possibility of compromise. It is only our pride which whispers that compromise is possible.

I weep for myself and for all of us. Oh Father! We live only by your Grace. Grant us the wisdom to know it.

The Golden Years

Golden years, my foot! The only gold I see is related to male urinary incontinence. Everything that still works hurts and I'm none too happy about it, but the thing I resent the most is the loss of my cohort. When I was a young man, I had friends with whom I could discuss my idle thoughts. Then, when I retired, a new community formed at the Chapel of St. Arbuck's, a cohort we titled "The Romeo Club". Romeo, given our ages, stood for Retired Old Men Eating Out.

As did those with whom I worked when I was younger, the people in the Romeo Club shared both interests and perspectives. We were all within 15 years of age of each other. Our memories were formed in a world much different than the one within which we found ourselves living. We shared alarm over the future, and affection for our memories.

Then, we began losing members. One died. One just drifted away. It continued that way until the Romeo Club had but two members. Then, even that died away as the last other member told me clearly that I was a burden and that he was no longer interested in our conversation.

Did you have a relative who sat at home alone? Did you visit him or her out of charity and try to look interested at his stories of life before you were born? Were you bored out of your skull? Of course you were. You shared nothing with him and his stories were repetitious. Old people are burdensome even to other old people.

This, I think, is why I get morose sometimes, quite apart from my distress over the urinary incontinence thing. I need company, but not just people. I need someone who can share the fields which gave bloom to me, people who might remember with me building a go-cart powered by a Maytag gasoline washing machine motor, not someone to whom I must explain that there was a time when washing machines ran on gasoline.

And there are very few such people left. I think that is why I write idle thoughts on Facebook. It's not as good as a meeting of the ROMEO Club, but it gives me the mirage of a conversation with those who enjoy my presence.

Forgive an old man for whining.

Meaning

A few days ago I posted this question on Facebook:

"There have been 234 mass shootings this year, 16 since last Saturday. The shooter at the light rail facility in San Jose had 22,000 rounds of ammo. That speaks of a terrified man. Can you name the terror he perceived?"

I simply can't accept that these people are as baffled by their actions as was Knowlt Hoheimer in Spoon River Anthology who speculated:

I was the first fruits of the battle of Missionary Ridge.
When I felt the bullet enter my heart
I wished I had stayed at home and gone to jail
For stealing the hogs of Curl Trenary,
Instead of running away and joining the army.
Rather a thousand times the county jail
Than to lie under this marble figure with wings,
And this granite pedestal Bearing the words, "Pro Patria."
What do they mean, anyway? [10]

I must have posed a good question because I got thoughtful answers. One respondent suggested fear of being erased. Another simply said, "Hate". One respondent said, correctly I think, that terror isn't rational.

I wanted to dig a little deeper and added, "I agree with all the foregoing but what do you think HE imagined the terror to be?" That did, indeed, uncover some deeper thinking. Deeper thinking is what we need if we are to understand what is so terrifying a portion of our community that they are led to actions of such

---

[10] Edgar Lee Masters, Spoon River Anthology

violence. As I read through the responses, two stood out. One commentator offered this:

I know nothing about the shooter. What I do know is what oppressors (homophobes, racists, etc.) fear most is that if the oppressed gain power, they are in for eye-for-an-eye justice, when in fact that almost never happens. The Klan rose up out of reconstruction to repel a threat that never materialized.

Well said! The response which most moved the wheels in my head, though, was this one:

"I think most of these shooters, who happen to be predominantly young, white and male, are experiencing a sense of existential dread. A hopelessness. No gainful employment, no living wage, no American Dream. For generations we told our young people "the sky is yours." "The world is your oyster." You only have to work hard, and you'll succeed." But work where? Fast food? Walmart? Even college graduates are working at Starbucks. They're lonely. They have no real connections. They work but can't save. They live in their parent's basement with no real prospect of owning a home or supporting a family. They despair and they are looking for a scapegoat…"

Ding! Ding! We have a winner, I think.

There is a painting of Christ knocking at a door which has no external latch. I think it is in every church I ever entered. The lesson is clear that Christ may not enter unless someone on the other side of the door opens it and invites him in. Bit heavy-handed, but a worthy message. Those young people my respondent spoke of are very like the image of Christ in the painting. They would knock on the door of the American dream, but someone has hidden the latch. There is no point of entry, and without such, there is no point in searching. Better to live in your parents' basement.

This will not do. I was hospitalized not long ago and it was horrific. I experienced, first hand, what being objectified will do to you. I was not consulted on a treatment plan. I was not informed of what was planned. It was plain to me that the hospital, once a place of healing, had become a corporate machine, a device which accepted injured or ill human beings as its raw material, processed that raw material to extract the nourishing insurance money from it, then discarded the remainder. When I became frustrated and demanded that I be treated with dignity, an LPN told me clearly that I had no right to talk to her or the staff in that way. I was to passively allow the machine to chew me until all the nourishment had been extracted. How can people trying to find their way in such an economy NOT become frustrated? Perhaps, instead of asking why we have so many mass shootings we might inquire why we don't have more?

Belittlement

I encountered the "nobody wants to work" excuse the other day. So the theory goes, the government pays people not to work, so employers with jobs can't fill them. Well, on one level, that may be so, but as the meme would have it, saying that the government stimulus package encourages people not to work is another way of saying you are paying starvation wages. On many more levels that is also correct.

I found myself hearkening back to my childhood in the 1950's. Ashland wasn't a particularly hostile place for people of color so long as those of color kept their distance. Any attempt to move up the social scale by taking a good paying job was seen as "taking" a good paying job from one of "us". Then, when those of color were well placed in the lowest of the low paying jobs, we white residents could look upon their squalor in Avondale, for instance, and note that people of color were too lazy to work to improve their lot.

The same thing is happening today, but the demarcation isn't along racial lines but upon corporate ones. Today the real power lies with corporations who do not bear their fair share of taxation, who take care to minimize the line item cost of "labor", and who can value only an accounting book, for things such as respect, love and family are outside their ken. To the sight of a corporation, young adults living in the basements of their parents' home is evidence that they are lazy. Like our population of color in my childhood, if they only would work hard at the jobs they are offered, they would succeed.

This is the American Creed. Education, hard work and a positive attitude leads, inevitably, to success. Anyone who fails, absent a readily discernible handicap, failed because of laziness or other character flaw. Such an explanation handily explains both

Avondale and unemployed young people without requiring any examination of the underlying assumption.

We know that is not so. We know that people with college degrees are working at Starbucks. We know that they incurred debt which will not be paid in a lifetime upon our assurance that they could assure themselves of success by seeking an education.

When we abandoned the slander that "Negros are lazy", we elected an African American as President and he served two terms. The same thing must happen for laborers, but in many ways the challenge is of a different degree.

A new predator stalks our amber fields of grain, one of our own creation. It is a legal fiction known as "the corporation". The corporation, though not a person, is granted many of the same rights as a person, but we have devised ways to free it from the responsibilities of a person. They, and their servants, are not required to bear their share of taxation for the good of the community. As a result, they use their extra resources to affect the democratic process beyond that which mere humans are able to do. The foundations are being laid for an automaton democracy, a horror which feeds upon humanity and excretes money for the amusement of its servants. To the degree to which we permit it, our mere human lives will descend to lower and lower advantage until we see another revolution. The recent violence may, in fact, be the beginning of such an uprising.

Johnny

My life as a young adult was a folly and a fraud. I learned how to kiss a girl from my high school sweet heart for I had no other experience. Then, after a number of years of dating, we eloped for a secret wedding in Virginia to which no family or friends were invited. This folly granted us permission to have intercourse within the demands of her faith. For my part, I was still trying to think with my testicles. As the history of humanity shows adequately, these organs are not up to the task of critical thinking.

The result was my son, John.

He was a cute little bugger, as you can see. Also, as you can see, I was a bit intense. Well, that's not surprising. If it had not been for my family's generosity, Johnny would have been the end of my career, but my family provided us housing and a living while I got through law school. Can you imagine such an act of self-denial?

Time passed and Johnny got a bit of education, though school wasn't his strong point. He moved to Louisville to be near his mother for at this point I had proved to be an unfaithful husband and she ran me out. She was right to do that.

So, I visited with John on alternate weekends, and tried to understand his life, with little success, for I was too young and inexperienced to be an effective father. We made it work, somehow and enjoyed a good relationship when we saw each other.

At one point, I volunteered at Appalshop, in Whitesburg, as an announcer for "From the Roots" on WMMT radio, the best little radio station in the whole wide world. Since my little brother had taken the radio name, "The Flying Dutchman", I became "The Old Dutchman". Truthfully, I had a ball pretending to be a DJ.

After a couple of years, John came to Ashland and said he'd like to go with me to see what I did on the radio. I agreed with enthusiasm. We had a great drive to Whitesburg, catching up on his life and mine. It was wonderful, frankly. I had grown into a man who could have a relationship with his son, and he was now a young man who could enjoy it as well.

On the way, we saw cars pulled off on the side. I could see no wreck, but pulled over as well. Johnny got out of the car before I did. As I emerged, John called, "Look Dad! Deer!" He pointed to the other side of the road. I looked.

In amazement, I replied, "Not deer, John. Elk!" Sure enough, there was a herd of elk there. The state had imported elk into Kentucky to replace the herds which once filled it. We were blessed by seeing them, and I lack the words to describe what a glorious sight they were.

I never did learn if John was as moved as was I. I did my shift while he explored Whitesburg. I don't recall any conversation about the elk on the way back but I was so moved.

That was the last time I saw my son.

John returned to Louisville and I returned to my lawyerly duties. We'd had our moment, and I was grateful, but life must go on. There are bills to be paid, both his and mine.

Sometime later, I don't recall how much later, the telephone rang. The voice on the line identified himself as Officer Someone of the Louisville Police Department. He said he had bad news about John. Johnny had been found dead in his bed.

His mother and I met to arrange that which required arranging. She told me that she preferred that no autopsy be performed for there is heart disease in my family and an autopsy might reveal things best not revealed. I agreed with her.

We cleaned out Johnny's apartment, the two of us. We didn't find evidence of drug use. I was glad of that, but from then to the end of my law enforcement career, I wept internally for those who must bury their children who died from overdose.

The Regular Way

In November, 1885, a baby boy was born on a farm near Fon du Lac, Wisconsin. His first priority, as with all children, was to understand the strange place into which he was born. Those early lessons will form for him the "regular way", the aggregate of his unspoken expectations of what the world is like. Is it a kind place? Is it a dangerous place? He was my grandfather, John Jacob Schneider, known as JJ, and by any measure he was a successful man for we are still living on some of the money he made.

But, had he been born 30 years later, the regular way would have been much different. He might have encountered anti-German feelings generated by the First World War, for he spoke only German until high school. The regular way is tied to place and time. The regular way is also tied to those guiding a child, for the regular way is how racism and other cultural slanders are transmitted, generation to generation.

Before he could become the successful man he would become, life offered JJ an appalling challenge. His father, Johannas Nicholas Schneider, the immigrant, died when he was only 15. He went to work for a nearby farmer to support his family and did so well that the farmer paid for a college education for the boy with no father. For him, that was a part of the regular way – commitment to responsibilities, even unsought ones, kindness to others and community response to bereavement.

What young JJ knew of the regular way he knew because he lived it. Nobody told him what the regular way might be. He discovered it for himself through living it. That, I would assert, is not the way those of my generation and later learned of their regular way. We learned through movies and television, and the world portrayed in movies and television was worlds apart from that lived by young JJ. The world portrayed in movies and television is plot-driven and to be successful requires characters drawn with the broadest possible strokes. For my generation and younger, the regular way is peopled with good guys and bad guys. There is no path for redemption of bad guys. There is no temptation for good guys. All is black and white. For those born into this regular way, it is wise to be armed, for the bad guys could appear at any time.

In place of the nuanced and nourishing regular way JJ knew, a place where a neighbor would take responsibility for the education of an orphaned neighbor's child, we have been fed a junk-food diet of fictional caricatures that leads us to see villains on every street corner. The shooter at the rail yard recently had 22,000 rounds of ammunition, and a California judge recently ruled that an AK-47, a military weapon designed to spread death as widely and quickly as possible was "an ideal home defense weapon". Only to move a television plot line would anyone even think anything that daft.

The Man on Central

At my age, it sometimes seems that what stretches before me is a lingering farewell to color and love, flavors and joy, family and friends. These were my thoughts as I sat in a parking lot near the hospital, waiting for my mother-in-law to finish her therapy.

"What is life if the opportunity to create something, gain something, accomplish something is gone forever?", I thought. A movement on the street caught my eye.

Across Central was a man of a certain age, a backpack, that identifier of the homeless, on his back. His hair, now a hedge row around the back of his head was, no doubt thick and full at one time. Now, his bare scalp was being rained on, but he didn't seem to notice it. His legs, which must have carried him through the joys of childhood were now damaged and he walked with a marked limp. Limp or no limp, he proceeded on his way. The rain came harder now, but his pace remained the same, slowed by the limp, but unhurried by a desire to escape the rain.

"There I go", I thought. "Old and worn out with no purpose left." Something told me to consider what was before my eyes more closely. The man I was watching clearly had no purpose apart from existence. His backpack was his home. His hair would never return. His life was at the mercy of the rain and the cold and he at the mercy of others, but none of that changed the regularity of his pace. He lived, it seemed to me, not to accomplish but merely to live. That was his purpose and it was enough.

I have been blessed.

Once, We Were Iron Masters

Once, we were iron masters, our faces illuminated orange and yellow from the fierce, fiery glow of ladles filled with unformed automobiles, bridge struts yet to be, the skeletons of buildings only dreamed of. We watched for the blast of Bellefonte and mighty Amanda. We managed the trains which brought the ore and limestone. We made coke in the coking ovens and managed trains that trundled it to the maw of Amanda over tracks that now lie concealed in weeds and grass, awaiting a train that will never come. We melted zinc and coated the iron we made with it, watching as the silver mirror cooled to crystal coating that the iron should not rust. We fed Amanda with the bones of Bellefonte, and left a gap. Now, we will do the same with Amanda and no child will ever see her again. Once, we were iron makers, strong of arm. What shall we be now?

Crazy Old Man

When I was a young man and heard stories on the news of old men just walking off and becoming lost, I mentally shrugged my shoulders and wrote it off to "crazy old man". Now, I'm a crazy old man in my 8th decade and I have come to see just where the crazy old men were going. They were seeking a time when railroad engines drew pictures in the sky with smoke and pulled cars in which people rode, a time when boats on the Ohio River were pushed by great wooden wheels with the power to walk on water.

I'm reminded of closing my cousin's estate, many years ago. Mary Lib had been a missionary in India. Her house was filled with mementos and antiques. She had place for every one and every one was in its place. They formed a record of her life. Now, they were taken down and arranged for the auctioneer's gavel. There her things stood, now ripped from living memory and the context in which they had been displayed, no longer part of a life story, now, merely assets. SOLD! the auctioneer shouted, and some memory moved from its rightful place to a new place as a tchotchke for the decoration of a stranger's night stand.

This is how I see my life now. In my mental knapsack are such memories as I have retained, some shameful, some shining. Some mundane but still representative of events in my life. When I go, these things, much too ephemeral for an auctioneer's gavel, will be gone in a puff. Will life on this small part of the earth be reduced by their loss? I cannot think so, yet I cling to them with passion and wander in search of what is now lost even to me.

After a lifetime of being useful, of supporting a family, of accomplishing things of value, old men must face a changed and frightening world, one in which we must be cared for. That's why we go searching for our comfort in the once and forever familiar.

The Principle of the Thing

The most powerful debate ending phrase known to the English speaking world is, "It's the principle of the thing". Once uttered by either side of a debate, the debate is over, for we are taught from childhood that principles are unassailable. Once one side (or both) of a debate announce that they speak in defense of "the principle of the thing" they have drawn a line in the sand, retreat from which would constitute abandonment of their principles, and with that, the debate is ended for it is no longer about the former subject of the debate but, rather, which side possesses the high moral ground. Compromise, growth, education are now all but impossible.

Walter Wink once noted, "One of the best ways to discern the weakness of a social system is to discover what it excludes from conversation." That stands as well for us as individuals for serious questions about the validity of our principles are automatically excluded from conversation. Our principles, then, can speak much about our intimate thoughts.

Moreover, our reverence for our personal unassailable principles demonstrates our preference for deleting meaning from important concepts, leaving but hollow shells to which we attach great loyalty. "I pledge allegiance to the flag..." No, I don't. The flag is a bit of cloth. I pledge allegiance to "the Republic for which it stands". Flags ask nothing more of us than formality. The Republic for which it stands demands of us loyalty to the principles from which it was formed, that all men are created equal, that they are endowed by their Creator with certain unalienable Rights, that among these are Life, Liberty and the pursuit of Happiness. This has been called "one of the best-known sentences in the English language", containing "the most potent and consequential words in American history". The passage represents the moral standard to which the United States should strive. Our weakness is revealed in our continual refusal to truly confront the ways our country has failed to live up to that standard, substituting for it empty words and fluttering flags.

Dr. Cathy Britell stated it most elegantly:

> **"The Flag and the Bible and Jesus and Guns mean different things to different people. To many these are all equally important magical "THINGS" that work as a talisman against unknown "EVILS" and allow people to proceed through their lives with less fear...of humiliation...of physical attack....even of dying."**

When we hear "It's the principle of the thing" enter a debate then we should understand, first, what is being feared? Why has this debate called forth the need for a talisman? Then, perhaps, the discussion might continue with greater understanding.

Rise of the Heron

Life speaks to us in language too nuanced for words. As we rounded a curve the parking lot for the college came into view. I paid it no attention, for what could draw my attention to a swath of sterile blacktop covering an area once filled with grasses and wild flowers, now neutered to human needs, a place to store one's automobile? As in so much which we touch, the life had been smothered from it, and it was no more than the backdrop of my trip to church, unworthy, in its sterility, of even a passing notice.

To its far end, however, is a swath of green beside Town Branch, the open sewer which once split Avondale, that refuge of the poorest of the poor. In Avondale those without hope raised life from little, life equally without hope but nevertheless, life. It was from that small patch of green that my eye caught, first, movement then a great upswing of wings as

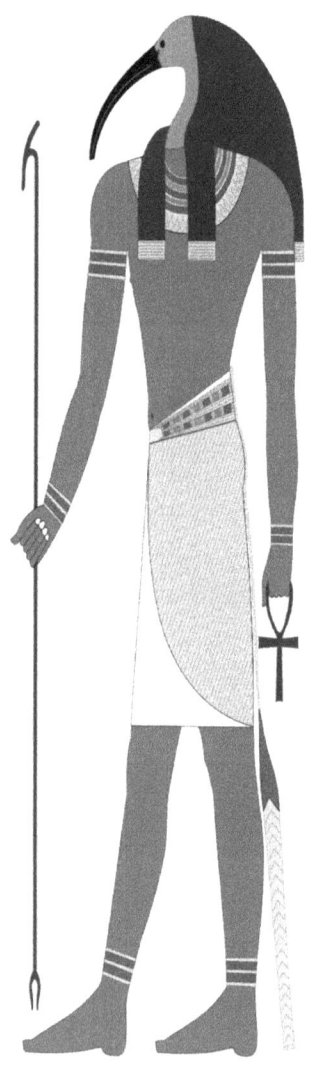

the head of Thoth rose on a wingspan of six feet or more, sailing first above the asphalt, then over the dividers, the god of wisdom, writing, hieroglyphs, science, magic, art, judgment, and the god of the dead, triumphant over the neutering efforts of man. With a single stroke the great heron soared directly over us, triumphant, for life speaks to us in language too nuanced for words.

The Adena

There is, on private land near Catlettsburg, an Adena serpent mound. We were speaking of it as we passed the Ashland Oil Refinery. It is odd to think that a structure from the Early Woodland Culture, perhaps 2,500 years old, could co-exist with so odd a thing as an oil refinery, but there it is. It started the wheels in my head.

Yesterday, the looming forest in which we live, the same forest hunted by the Adena so many years past presided implacably over Ashland, contemptuous of our noise and nonsense and from it came voices from the past. "We came before you", they seem to say. "We lived within this forest you have tried, unsuccessfully, to claim. It remains. You will pass as did we."

A Dead Cat

Driving 13th Street, Stan Rogers was singing "The Last Watch on the Midland", a sad song of a sailor hired to stand watch over a ship in the boneyard on, "the last night she's whole". Old men think of the end of things for our long lives grant us permission to see the end of things clearly for what they are. Rogers' song suited my mood as I thought on what it means to be alive.

Science teaches us that the insensate universe somehow pulls itself into organization to walk unaided about in it, even to think on its loveliness and to ponder the end of things. An odd collection of fibers and stones, and atoms of this and that somehow becomes organized into you and me that we might occupy ourselves pondering these things and others.

Just then, around a curve, I saw something in the roadway. It appeared to be the wreck of a house cat, smeared and smashed by a car which the cat, for want of attention had not seen, or had not been quick enough to escape. There it was, all the collection of atoms which had once been a cat, its organization now ruined, and with it, the essence of the cat.

Stan Rogers sang,
"The last watch on the Midland
The last watch alone.
One more night to love her
The last night she's whole."

Then, as I drew nearer, I saw that what I had taken for the wreck of a cat was really a piece of pink insulation, so never mind.

As the Twig is Bent

As the twig is bent so grows the tree. Those understandings we receive as children we take into ourselves uncritically, and they form the basis of our adult lives. They can be changed only with difficulty. It is the task of an adult mind, and the very definition of maturity to examine them. Two such matters came to mind today at lunch with my family – racial relations and law and order.

Here are the understandings of racial relations given me as a child: My grandfather lived at the top of Prospect hill. Behind the house was his "shop". Across the alley from his shop was his dump. Beside the dump was a path leading downward. We were not allowed to follow the path, but had we done so, we would have found ourselves on Oakview road, across from Avondale. Avondale was where the "coloreds" lived. We were not allowed to go there, for no expressly stated reason. Each morning, a quiet group of women emerged from the path beside the dump, then went down Prospect Avenue to work in the large houses on Lexington Avenue. In the evening, they retraced their steps, quietly.

Granddad once owned movie theatres. When I knew him, he owned nothing, but had a made-up job at the Capital Theater. We went with him on Saturday evenings. We boys wanted to sit in the balcony but were told strictly that it was not "structurally sound" and were forbidden to go there. Of course, this being the 1950's the truth was that the balcony was reserved for people of color. We did not know that nor were we even aware that there were people of color watching the same movies we watched. Such things were simply not discussed, again for no expressly stated reason.

Dr. Everett Moore, who lived across the street from my house, employed a housekeeper named Imogene. Each morning,

Imogene disembarked from a bus at Blackburn and walked two blocks to Dr. Moore's house. In the evening, she returned, boarding a bus to her home. We did not know where she lived. We did not know if she was married, or had children. She was silent, both ways, and we boys never interacted with her, on the street or on the rare occasions we were admitted to the Moore's house.

When my mother hosted a large party, she often hired Stella to help with the food preparation. I said "help" rather than "prepare" because my mother worked in the kitchen with her, elbow to elbow. Stella was a happy sort with an easy laugh and she and my mother worked well together. We were expected to be polite and respectful toward her, which was easy because she was a pleasant person. When the job was completed, Mom or Dad would drive her home, I believe on Sixth Street. I never recall encountering her on the streets, and do not know what would have been expected of me had that happened.

This is how our twigs were bent. People of color were not to be treated with hatred or contempt, but neither were they to be interacted with in any way. I was a grown man before I learned that Town Branch, the waterway that split Avondale, was, in actuality, an open sewer and that the houses in Avondale lacked sanitary sewers. The phrase is "benign neglect" but once the truth was learned, it is clear that there was nothing benign about it. People of color were treated as non-humans. It wasn't malicious or hate-driven. It was the perspective of the time for white people and accepted sotto voce, without analysis, or, indeed, any conscious awareness that it was happening. This was absorbed into my young mind without question as the way the world worked.

Law and order was another understanding I was given, but not by my parents. This came from comic books, movies and, later, television. For me, Batman and Robin formed a big part of this understanding. Gotham City was plagued with crime. It also had a large police department, but that police department seemed unable to address the darker forces which threatened the city. Oh, I suppose they were effective enough with the common run of criminals, but when big, scary evil appeared, they were at a loss, and when that happened, when evil seemed its most threatening, Commissioner Gordon flashed the Batsignal.

We didn't think too deeply about what made Batman so effective, so grateful were we to have him set the world right. Setting the world right was the important thing. Methods were details and we didn't bother our young heads over details. Batman's readiest weapon was that he had no need for due process or the rule of law. He could tie his Batrope where he chose. He could roar though the city in the Batmobile, free of the constraints of the traffic laws. Indeed, his primary effectiveness sprang, not from the endless gadgets in his Batbelt, but from his liberation from the constraints of the law. Batman don't need no stinkin' warrant. He could crash through the window with no consequences.

As I think back on these things, I can see how threatening was the evolution of our society to the understandings we received uncritically as children. The rise of Civil Rights demanded that people of color be seen as human beings, brothers and sisters to be engaged as such, not mute objects to be passed without notice, but we weren't brought up that way and to change the ways we were taught as children is difficult for any of us. Indeed, it seems no great stretch to see this evolution, this change in perspective, as not different from the big, scary evil which caused Commissioner Gordon to flash the Batsignal.

We can see in the armed militias on the streets at protest sites the echo of Batman's extra-legal actions in the name of order. The same need for order which lead Commissioner Gordon to flash the Batsignal now lead policemen to offer bottles of water to armed 17 year old Kyle Rittenhouse, who was playing army in a town a state away from his home, and to thank him for his help. Yes, we need order in the streets, but we must have law as well. That point was not given me as a child.

These are the cultural norms our childhoods gave us, the shibboleths with which we grew up. People of color weren't to be treated badly; they were simply not to be acknowledged at all. The rule of law which imposes limits on the good as well as the bad empowers the forces of disorder so it is only to lawlessness that we can turn for protection from the poorly-defined but very frightening forces we feel now threaten our very existence. We are little inclined to think on these matters, because to challenge these holy things is to try to straighten a tree bent since youth. Such attempts bring forth pain in a society already steeped in great pain. It is more convenient to brand as evil that which would cause us to re-examine our bent twigs.

Unless we develop the courage to recognize the wisdom of our founders, and the courage to engage the forces of division, I weep for my country. It is not too late, but it is rapidly becoming so.

Pass the Potato Salad

We've had two weeks now of floating billionaires. That's remarkable. You'd think all that money would make them too heavy to float, but as it turns out, billionaires float just fine. Even more remarkable is that an 18 year old kid could pony up $26,000,000 to float for 3 minutes, after someone else bid $28,000,000 for the privilege then had to cancel when he realized he had a "scheduling conflict".

"No, wait. I take it back. I can't go. I've got that thing at the Biltmore that weekend." With that kind of money, he didn't have a calendar?

Then, this week at Starbuck's, I met a member of the Navajo Nation – a very nice lady with an adorable 5 year old daughter. We had a nice chat. She told me that she works for Sonic and was in town to do the dry walling and other work on the new Sonic. Sonic sends her all over the country to do this sort of work, and she goes with her daughter in tow. Then, she told me she had twins at home. Her husband stays with them while Sonic moves her around the country. I don't think she floats at all. Her life seems pretty challenging to me.

For some in this great country money is life as it is to my Navajo friend. To others, it is a toy, something to amuse light-headed billionaires.

We can do it, you know. If we can blast billionaires into space for the fun of it, we can build an economy which feeds all. I hear the objection that this is a false equivalence. Floating billionaires are vastly different from hungry people, but what if we approached the problems of human misery with the same enthusiasm with which we approach the possibility of space tourism? How would it be if we didn't see the world as the field upon which we battle each other for wealth, but as a church picnic? How would it be if we just passed the potato salad?

Two Cents Worth

Framed on the desk in my study are two pennies I found on a parking lot, one atop the other. They are a sight. Scratched up, kicked around, abused, but I had them framed, just as I found them, one heads up, the other tails. They are on my desk because they made me wonder about their history.

On the street, nobody would bother to pick them up, they have so little value. They aren't part of "proof set" sealed in plastic.

Indeed, they never even made a transaction by themselves; they were just there to complete a transaction, to pay the sales tax.

On the other hand, if it weren't for the penny, the bookkeeping would be an impossible snarl. That's a pretty big deal, when you think of it. Its presence isn't valued, but its absence would have enormous consequences.

Almost everything that happened to the pennies wasn't their fault, but what happened to them left marks upon them. The history of those two pennies changed them, and made them unique. A proof set penny, on the other hand, is sterile and indistinguishable from any other proof set penny. Coin collectors might value it but it brings nothing with it. I like my two cent's worth. That's why they have a place of honor on my desk.

Very Fine People

Another idle thought...

I think when Trump said, of Charlottesville, that "there were very fine people on both sides", he said more than he knew. I know people who now support Trump – people I have known for years and who I respect. Does Trump's "base" contain white supremacists, racists, and dimwits? Yes, sadly, it does. Are all Trump supporters white supremacists, racists and dimwits? Of course not. Many are very fine people, people I have known and interacted with, finding them sound. My friend, Pamela, posted a meme which asserted

"For me, personally, the most painful aspect of Trump's rise has been the damage it has caused to my faith in my fellow Americans. I do not understand how a person can watch what he says and does and still think he belongs in the Oval Office."

This is my problem, precisely. How can people in whom I believe, people I have dealt with and found to be of sound judgment, watch the horror show which the White House has become and still be unmoved? Pamela's posting frames the problem precisely. How do I reconcile an evaluation of soundness reached after years of interacting with people I know well with a support for this dangerous villain? I am at a loss, and yet, I am not willing to discard people I like to the trash bin. I want to understand.

When I ask, though, I am often called "hater". I do not hate this man. I fear him. I fear the damage he is doing and will do to the country I love. When I ask, I am told it's "just my opinion", which is no answer at all. When I ask, I am directed to numbers about the economy, but the economy has crashed due to inept response to the virus. Finally, when all else is exhausted, I am told "abortions", as if that resolved all doubts. If I then quote C. S. Lewis and offer,

"The most dangerous thing you can do is to take any one impulse of your own nature and set it up as the thing you ought to follow at all costs. There is not one of them which will not make us into devils if we set it up as an absolute guide." I am again branded a hater and worse for my failure to stand up for my faith.

A few weeks ago, I was criticized by someone who reads my sermons online for preaching about contemporary failures of our people to walk the walk Jesus showed us. "Why don't you preach against homosexuality or killing unborn babies?" was the charge. That's an odd grouping, and the only connection I can see between these two things is that they represent things my critic could never imagine happening in her life. Then, during my studies, I found the explanation I sought, ..."A large percentage of humanity has little self-knowledge and project most of their evil elsewhere. They never struggle with their shadow self in any real sense, but just try to think of themselves as moral and right, at all costs. Remember again Jesus' great one-liner, "Because you say, 'I see,' your guilt and blindness remain" (John 9:41).[11] It is understandable in the young boy. It is abhorrent and sad in the old man".

I fear that may offer a solution. Trump offers "the other" as the villain. Our economic problems are the result of illegal aliens. Our manufacturing ills are because of the Chinese. It is always someone else's fault. We are the victims of "the other" and only a strong man, like Trump, stands between us and "the other". One cannot read such trash without thinking of Mussolini, yet my friends do not see the similarities. Instead, they cling with straining sinews to their picture of themselves as moral and good, closing their eyes tightly to any examination of their shadow self. Was I foolish enough to point that out, I am certain that the response would be, "You're doing the same thing". For

---

[11] Richard Rohr, "From Wild Man to Wise Man"

the followers of Trump, there seems no truth, no morality, no measure of integrity – only opinion.

I do not like this explanation. It denigrates my friends, and I'm loyal to them. I want an explanation which allows me to view my friends in a positive light, and to see our differences as only good-faith differences of opinion. I have, so far, been unable to find such a path.

Right Wing/Left Wing

I'm outraged by lawyer ads. Whether it's the "We're the biggest because we win a lot" or the even more insidious "We know how to turn an elderly relative in a care home into cold, hard cash", any of these obscenities would have cost me and my colleagues trying to be professionals our cards. The Bar Association once enforced professional behavior. Today, it's every man for himself. It rankles me.

It was, therefore, with celebration that I listened to one of those same colleagues, after losing a serious criminal case, explain on television that, "The jury felt that under the evidence and the court's instructions, this was the correct verdict. You have to trust the system." All honor to you, Frenchie.

On the other side of the spectrum, a classmate since grade school wrote in response to positive comments in support of a single payer health care system that she "didn't want the government to be in charge of her health care".

On the one hand, we have an experienced professional who has dedicated his life to serving within the American system of justice and who has learned, by that experience, to trust the unique thing America's justice system is even when he has lost a case. He didn't lose his case because the system is corrupt. He lost his case precisely because the system worked correctly.

On the other hand, my classmate, a straight-A student as I recall, posts right-wing talking points on Facebook frequently and without any evident fact-checking, the burden of which is that the system IS corrupt and never to be trusted. That same classmate and others like her would, I'm sure, be "proud to be an American, where at least I know I'm free". For those on that side of the spectrum, "free" means anarchy, every man for himself, the demands of the one outweigh the needs of the many, a thought space in which self is idolized without any leavening of responsibility towards others.

> **"Adam, where are you?" (cf. Gen 3:9). Where are you, o man? What have you come to? ...Who corrupted you? Who disfigured you? Who led you to presume that you are the master of good and evil? Who convinced you that you were god? Not only did you torture and kill your brothers and sisters, but you sacrificed them to yourself, because you made yourself a god.** [12]

_____

[12] Pope Francis, 26 May 2014

Living Within the Minute

We had a great time in Lexington, and because the Farmer's Market was on, there were street musicians. I struck up a conversation with a very old set of whiskers who had a slide guitar, a harp and a fiddle. He told me he was 75 and without thinking, I replied that I am as well. That's technically not true. I won't finish my 75th year up for 2 more months, but it's close enough for Bluegrass as they say.

One of my old friends used to tell me quite often that he lives within the minute and doesn't worry about the future, nor regret the past. In particular he told me he doesn't worry about dying because, he reasons, he will have lost interest at that point. I can see the value of his words, but as I confessed to my age, another thought crossed my mind. How can you "live within the minute" while cutting yourself off from the experiences, regrets included, which brought you to this minute? How can you live within the minute without embracing the anxieties which will bend your course to the next minute without feeling adrift, alone upon a dark sea?

I never had the knack to live "within the minute" and the more I think on it, the more grateful I become. Living within the minute (and my friend's corollary that the minute must be enjoyed to the fullest) seems to me more like a child demanding dessert, dessert and nothing but dessert. Life, lived fully, contains both great joy and sadness and if there is a trick to living life it is to embrace its fullness.

Or, perhaps as my friend insists, I'm just looking for trouble.

Sookie

Too good not to share. But first, you must understand the geography. Our couch has three cushions. One for Kathy, one for me and the center cushion which is claimed by Sookie. Sookie is a big, long dog, so when she gets all stretched out, her head is in my lap and her back legs are pushing Kathy against the side of the couch.

Sometimes, it's just too crowded so I'll move to a recliner and she'll stretch into my space. Such was the case last night. When Kathy saw what had happened, she said, "Sookie! That's not very nice! Your daddy needs a place to sit."

If I hadn't seen it with my own eyes, I wouldn't believe it but that dog lifted her head, looked at me with apologetic big brown eyes, got off the couch, walked to Kathy's side, jumped up and rolled herself into a tiny ball, small enough to fit on her cushion. I swear that dog understands English!

The Eve of Destruction

The more I think on my unsatisfactory engagements with insurance and bank corporations, the more convinced I become that human values have been engulfed by the single-minded pursuit of profit. I'm also coming to be convinced that the devaluation of purely human values like pride of workmanship by the machine that is our computer-driven economy, is one of the most toxic elements of contemporary life for those of us with some mileage on our odometers. As an example, I offer the automated phone system.

The most reliable way to set off a cranky old man is to connect him with any sort of automated phone system that instructs him to press 1 for hours of operation, 2 for billing and so on, then, when he's made his choice, tell him to please hold for the next available agent and play him music designed specifically to drive him away. That will do it. We're already aware that we are no more than an inconvenience to the young people who live within the computerized environment that is our world. We don't need to be reminded.

I have recently had two encounters with the soul-sucking automatons of our time – banks and insurance companies – due to the unwelcome entry of a large tree into the space formerly known as "my home". In February a sudden freeze dropped trees all over my part of the country. It was late enough that the sap had begun to rise in the trees, but sudden enough that the sap froze solid, exploding the tree trunks like hand grenades, causing the trees to topple over, obliterating anything in their way. My house was in the way.

I do not know which was the more difficult to deal with – the bank, the insurance company, or the tree. Oh, ye innocent souls who would speak reason to such brutal leviathans do not go down to the dark waters where lives the Kraken. Rather, remove your hat, tug upon your forelock and offer up, meekly, your money, your humanity, and your self-esteem.

Those of us who grew up in a time when economic transactions were between human beings, rather than through electronic intermediaries resent the impersonal nature of such transactions. Rather than the "Hey! What can I do for you?" to which we accustomed ourselves in the naive years of our youth, we get "Push 1 for hours of operation" and it offends us older ones who hunger for the nourishment of human contact once offered, even in trivial economic transactions. The message we receive is that individual customers are as worthy of note as individual drops of water in a mill stream are to the mill wheel. We are the anonymous drips which power the machinery but are otherwise unworthy of note.

Following one such frustrating encounter, I left fuming for another appointment. I arrived much too early, and pulled up facing the side of a building, then set my iPhone to play the folk music of the 1960's. I needed comfort, but then the burlesque of the situation struck me. I was sitting there, listening to the music of a more nourishing time of my existence, while facing an impenetrable brick wall, the image of my future. The iPhone was playing, "You tell me over and over again, my friend. You don't believe we're on the eve of destruction."

For that time, I believed. My home was a wreck. Something needed to happen without the intervention of any buttons at all.

That looked pretty hopeless. I needed someone or something which could give me reason to hope. My rescuer arrived the form of an old family friend who runs a contracting business specializing in home building and remodeling. Now we're talking. This is the way it used to be, the way that fits my expectations.

And it was so. The work was done by actual craftsmen who understood what they were doing and insisted on doing what they understood. I was astounded and gratified. This is how it is supposed to be – pride of workmanship unalloyed by the ravening Kraken of corporate profit.

For the next six months or so, the remains of the tree, which we named "Randall the Vandal", glared at us as we watched TV.

Glare away, old villain. Glare away!

The Lug Nut Key

So far, in the past month or six weeks, I have experienced three eruptions. That's not good. The first was with Spectrum. I wanted them to put a residential account at the church because we don't do enough on the net to justify a business account. They refused. I became angry, demanding to know why they wouldn't do so simple a thing. They became aggressive. I erupted.

The second was Fifth-Third Bank. We had canceled Kathy's debit card for fear of an attack upon it, and the bank issued a pre-paid card to get us through until the replacement card arrived. Then a replacement card arrived. It was declined when she tried to use it. Turns out that instead of a debit card, it was another pre-paid card and we hadn't loaded any money on it. I called the bank and was connected to a computer answering system. I was instructed to press 1 for English and 6 for something else and asked for my social security number and given a nasal swab and I don't recall what else, then was provided some music so vile that I cannot describe it. I felt the magma rising and in a blind fury, I drove to the bank. That's what old people do. We go to the bank to talk to a bank manager. There are no bank managers in banks anymore, I learn. There are young women at whom you can shout incoherently, but their answer always is the same: I didn't do that, and I can't do anything about it. Here's what I can do...

I grew up knowing bank presidents. Hell, my grandfather WAS one. You went to the bank, the manager or the president greeted you by name and had the power to get done what you needed. I erupted at the young woman so badly that the following day I had to send her flowers to apologize.

The final eruption was the worst, by far. Kathy's tire went flat and we called AAA. A man in a truck arrived in due course, confirmed that the tire was indeed flat and asked me for "the key". I handed him my key ring.

"No", he said. "I need the lug nut key."

The lug nut key. I had been taking my nap when the tire went flat. I had been awakened so far by three automated phone calls telling me the man was on his way, one knock at the door which sent the dog into hysterics when he arrived, and now a second knock to ask for the "lug nut key". The fuse was lit. The earth trembled and shook. A great plume of ash and smoke rose into the sky. I have never heard of a lug nut key. In a profanity-laced tirade unbecoming to a clergyman I told the man that I expected him to arrive with the tools he needed to do the work. He told me it isn't a tool. It's part of the car. By this time, the magma flowed with such force that my words were not, in any intelligible way, English.

So, what DID happen here? I'm a geezer. I subsist on the older, staler air of a time long past. Once, I could overcome barriers. Now I am confined by speed bumps. Once, I was important. Now, I am irrelevant. Once, I could grasp the challenges life presented me. Now, I'm baffled, and I'm mad as HELL about it! Don't connect me with computer answering devices that underline of how little importance I am to you. Greet me by name. Don't treat me as yet another impotent old person who needs to be helped up on the curb and directed out of the way as soon as possible. And for the love of humanity, FIX THE DAMN TIRE!

Suffering

I never met a football fan or a basketball fan. Oh, I know plenty of UK fans and some Cardinal fans, but a basketball or football fan, someone who appreciates the game itself apart from partisan considerations is a stranger to me. Truth is, I was never an athletic kid and that means I never had the experience of being a team player. Sometimes, that grieves me. Other times, not so much. The current border dispute in Texas is one of the "not so much" occasions. Without the experience of being a team player, I have no experience of team loyalty, you see.

Being foreign to team loyalty has followed me my entire life, so the heat generated over the issue of the border and particularly focusing on the people under the bridge in Texas, leaves me appalled. I can't grasp the idea that the suffering of someone not on my team is less important. A posting on Facebook by a friend of much more conservative bent than I caused this old Lion to whimper. Here's what he proudly posted:

> **I'll start caring about the struggles of illegal aliens when all 39,471 homeless veterans living in America are well fed, well sheltered and well taken care of.**

Well, I suppose that you could grant that some degree of reasonableness at first glance – a differing view, perhaps, but reasonable enough, until you start thinking about why compassion should be rationed in that way? Why should the suffering of veterans and the suffering of those under the bridge be in competition? Had two kids fallen simultaneously off different swing sets on the Oakview Grade School playground, I'd probably have run to help the nearest one first, but I wouldn't ignore the other one on the grounds he was one of the "other swing set people".

In the book of Numbers, we read about the wandering in the wilderness. That's a pretty good analogy for what the people under the bridge had been through before they reached Texas. They knew where they were going, but I don't think they anticipated border patrol agents on horseback whipping them, conduct that the chief of the border patrol called "shocking" and the vice-president said reminded her of tactics "used against the Indigenous people of our country" and "used against African Americans during times of slavery."

> Moses heard the people weeping throughout their families, all at the entrances of their tents. Then the Lord became very angry, and Moses was displeased. So Moses said to the Lord, "Why have you treated your servant so badly? Why have I not found favor in your sight, that you lay the burden of all this people on me? Did I conceive all this people? Did I give birth to them, that you should say to me, 'Carry them in your bosom, as a nurse carries a sucking child,' to the land that you promised on oath to their ancestors? Where am I to get meat to give to all this people? For they come weeping to me and say, 'Give us meat to eat!' I am not able to carry all this people alone, for they are too heavy for me.

Moses sounds an awful lot like those in our time who endorse building border walls and flying people who have spent months wandering the wilderness back to a country in crisis. The difference is that Moses, an individual, felt he could not carry all this people whereas we, a wealthy country, can do something to alleviate the suffering presented to us.

Finding the suffering of one on the other team to be acceptable is foreign to my way of thinking, not because of personal virtue but because that part of my childhood development, when such behavior was learned, is a blank for me. That's why I responded so strongly to the photo of Charles City, Iowa wide receiver Mario

Hoefer who ran to help a player on the other team who was down with a serious leg cramp. The media called it "sportsmanship" I see it as an image for life, a goal to be sought earnestly.

The Will to Wonder

This Saturday's discussion at the Chapel of St. Arbuck veered into the topic of signs and wonders. I'm unashamedly a signs and wonders kind of person. I find significance in dreams, in the odd people who cross my path, in all that goes on around me.

For my part, I am committed to my signs and wonders. I cannot escape the conviction that the world is more than a problem to be solved. Indeed my childhood experiences in the Capitol Theater left me with the conviction that those matters which bear so heavily upon us are little more than pictures cast upon a tattered screen.

But now, such talk, even in the Chapel of St. Arbuck, sounds hopelessly romantic. I wish for a return to wonder but fear that we have stamped the life from that possibility. Where now do we go for the will to wonder?

Abraham Joshua Heschel wrote:

> **"As civilization advances, the sense of wonder almost necessarily declines. Such decline is an alarming symptom of our state of mind. Mankind will not perish for want of information; but only for want of appreciation. The beginning of our happiness lies in the understanding that life without wonder is not worth living. What we lack is not a will to believe but a will to wonder."** [13]

---

[13] Man Is Not Alone: A Philosophy of Religion (Abraham Joshua Heschel)

The Hands of the Potter

I was preparing a sermon around a familiar verse from Trito-Isaiah:

> **"Yet, O Lord, you are our Father;**
> **we are the clay, and you are our potter;**
> **we are all the work of your hand."**

Out of nowhere, I hit a good lick and wrote:

> **"We have to pay attention to the potter's hands. Did someone say something today that was meaningful to you? That's the hands of the potter. Did you see something today that brought the love of God out of the shadows for you? That's the hands of the potter you saw. Did you become aware of someone else's need, and decide to fulfill them, maybe without even letting them know? You have become the hands of the potter."**

As I wrote, I was reminded of a peculiar event at Oakview Grade School. Mr. Pickleseimer, our terrifying principal, imperiously entered my 3rd grade classroom at Oakview Grade School in his accustomed black suit. Mr. Pickleseimer was not a person to be trifled with. Indeed, wise children avoided him at all cost, for fear of the electric paddling machine all children knew was in his office. He was also not by nature an affectionate man, given to delivering commands to be carried out without question or comment.

"Stewart", he said, looking directly at me. "From now on you will be released from class early for lunch. You will go to the cafeteria and do what Mrs. Barber directs, and you won't have to pay for your lunch."

Having spoken his piece, he turned on his heel and left.

For the younger people you should know that a school lunch at Oakview Grade School cost 30¢. A half pint of milk cost an additional 3¢. Such an expenditure did not, in any way, strain the resources of my family. Indeed, my father was vice president of the milk company, founded by his father, which provided the milk.

In hindsight, of course, it's easy to see that the announcement was a simple mistake. He had confused my name with the name of some child who needed a free lunch. Had I been a bit older, perhaps old Picklepuss's announcement would have been received with outrage. What did he mean by announcing in front of the whole class that my folks couldn't afford a 33¢ lunch for me? Surprisingly, I did not hear his words as a slight on my family. What I heard was that I, and only I, had been chosen from all the other children to be entrusted with this responsibility and, on top of that, I was to be paid, in the form of a free lunch, for my work. I received old Picklepuss's error as a favorable commentary upon my worth as a human being, not as a slight to my family.

The next day I was released from class and sent to the cafeteria. While the other students labored through arithmetic or social studies, I was freed of all that for I had work to do...work of such importance that it freed me from whatever drudgery the others suffered. I went through the halls and down the steps to the cafeteria with wings on my feet! After receiving my free lunch, I was directed behind the counter. BEHIND it! Where none but staff were permitted! No longer student, I was now staff!

My position as dishwasher continued throughout the 3rd grade. I recall being disappointed, when I entered 4th grade, to learn that my services were no longer required. With regret I sank back into the hoi polloi. Had I seen the hands of the potter?

Purpose and recognition are the bread and butter of our emotional lives. I passed a beggar on the corner. He was holding a neatly-lettered cardboard sign identifying himself as homeless and asserting that "anything will help". Unfortunately for him, I noticed as I passed that behind the sign, he was texting someone on a smart phone. I suppose the correct reaction would be to ascribe laziness and corruption to him, but I didn't quite get there. Instead, I saw someone who had never been granted the blessings of a purpose. Was he, I wondered, the son of the student who needed the free lunch I had gotten? Today, at Kroger, I passed three ranks of self-serve checkouts. That is three ranks of families whose purpose has been swallowed by a machine in the name of convenience. What of their purpose? Where, in the welfare line, do you locate your sense of self-worth and value?

Sermon Ex Tempore

Yesterday began as not a good day for me to be a preacher. My confidence collapsed. It ended better.

"What do you think you're doing, boy?" the voice in my head was asking as I prepared the sermon. I slogged on and finished the draft. "Good lesson", I thought, figuring that should be sufficient. That's when the voice in my head spoke in correction. Jesus' lesson IS sufficient. What arrogance to imagine I might improve upon it!

"What <u>do</u> you think you're doing, boy?", I heard the voice again as I looked out at my tiny congregation before service. My son-in-law was on his phone. My daughter was looking after the kids. Each congregant had filed to their accustomed spot, the spot which was theirs when the sanctuary was filled so many decades ago, which meant that they were scattered thinly about the pews, but that normality was assured. God was in His heaven and all, for this time, was right with the world. What did I think I was doing?

The service began and we came to the time of Confession. Presbyterians confess silently and it is my custom to introduce this time of introspection with a few words on the need to face up to those things we have done less well than we might have done. That is my custom but what came out of my mouth was, "This is the time we can go to the Lord and discuss his will for us."

Where did that come from? The voice in my head began sounding strained and asked, "What are you playing at, boy?" as I turned the page of the bulletin to the Prayer of Confession which the church secretary copies from some website and began to read.

> **"Gracious God, so often we look at our gifts and our talents and wonder what you would do with these offerings. We don't think that we have much to give, so**

we belittle the gifts and turn our backs on the needs and opportunities to serve, believing that we cannot possibly make a difference. We think that we must possess the greatest of talents and wealth in order to truly please and serve you. How foolish we are! Forgive us when we stop listening to your healing and comforting words and focus on our anxieties. Help us know that you have given to us these blessings that are meant to be used in service to others. Help us to bring our lives to you and to receive your gentle touch and healing grace."

The voice of condemnation I had heard all week had fallen silent. A sermon speaks to those most in need of hearing it.

Memories' Shadows

Old men spend too much time in regret. We remember those times which passed without appreciation, those momentous moments which flew by without being granted time to appreciate their importance. Only later, when the time has passed, do we find the memories of such times and events replayed before us with naught but regret to fill the emotional vacuum we allowed when younger.

For me, such memories generally center on my grandparents. My maternal grandparents were not successful people. My grandmother was addicted to morphine and mostly sat on the couch smoking cigarettes. My grandfather, son of a saloon keeper, was an impractical man who took little resource from the world, but gave much love and attention to us, his children.

My paternal grandparents were the opposite. My grandmother was the daughter of a subsistence farmer. My grandfather, also, but by dint of pure stubbornness, he learned English, took a job, and so impressed his employer that the employer put him through college. From there, he began a dairy and a savings and loan. Grandfather Stewart cradled his grandchildren in his lap and fed them applesauce scrapped from an apple half by the blade of his old pocket knife. Grandfather Schneider invited us to Sunday dinner, served on the dining table, with silverware.

I've grown old and now I can see in my memories that both grandfathers offered me experiences of worth. What I wouldn't give now for an hour with Granddad Stewart in his shop where I could pay attention to his stories instead of looking about for some piece of machinery I might ask for. What I wouldn't give for an hour with Granddad Schneider to ask him about his childhood and the days before the century turned. Alas! All gone, beyond recall. Missed opportunities now only to be regretted.

And then, today, Christmas Day, I sat on the couch after speaking with my maternal cousin, Dennis, my last living relative of that time and I silently prayed. I did not pray to return to those times. I silently prayed that I might be aware of the minutes I allow to slip through my fingers even now, that I might make amends in my life today for the life I had allowed to pass without notice then.

It was at the conclusion of my prayer that my earth shifted. I doubt I can put it into words. I suddenly perceived myself and my wife as parts of a memory of regret held by my children and grandchildren in a world yet to come which I cannot imagine, nor yet experience. They were praying a prayer that they be allowed one more hour in Granddad Schneider's house – my house. They were praying a prayer of regret that they had paid insufficient attention to their experiences. The ache and agony I felt for them brought me immediately to tears and to my office to write of the experience before it passed from me.

I don't know what the lesson might be to take from this experience. Perhaps there is none. Perhaps the best that can be said is that in some way we all form the foundations for a future adult's memories and their regrets or celebrations. Let us now, while they are young, help them to see that life is fleeting and infinitely precious. Let that be our job in our old age for we can pass on little wisdom beyond that.

A Great Day

I need to brag about my day yesterday. Kathy and I were to have lunch at the Winchester, but I had to kill 20 minutes or so and went to the park to watch the fountains. In front of me was a couple at a picnic table, laughing at each other's jokes and obviously much in love. It wouldn't have drawn my attention so strongly but for her beautiful gray hair and his balding scalp. They were my age, and so much in love that as they rose to leave, I spoke to her from my car to say how very touched I was and how much I enjoyed watching them. She told me they both had been widowed after long marriages, had met and married in January of this year, so they were still on their honeymoon. I hope I never forget this.

Then, on to the Winchester where Kathy met me. We're a pair. There's no other description. We laughed and enjoyed each other's company (and a wonderful chicken taco) just as had the honeymooners. It was a great lunch.

Thursday being our date night, when I rose from my afternoon nap I asked her where she'd like to go for supper. She'd like to go to Rocco's and who wouldn't? My doc has gotten pissy about my A1C so I'm not allowed carbs. I told Erin, one of our favorite servers, and she produced some really spectacular salmon on Caesar salad. Delicious!

Just when I thought the day couldn't be any better, someone came up behind me and snapped my suspenders! It was Richard "Sonny" Martin, my long-time friend and school mate and once my boss. Sonny is unquestionably smarter than I ever was, much more successful than I, and a joy to be around – one of those people who can bring sun to even a dreary day. His sudden appearance was the topper on my Sundae.

Of course, since he has bested me in everything I ever attempted, I have to have something to rub his nose in, and it's Kathy. She was hired by the city to be my file clerk one summer when she was in college. We started dating. Sonny had to do the managerial thing and advise me that dating innocent young interns was not wise. I reciprocate whenever we meet by telling him how long Kathy and I have been married. 44 years. Bullseye!

Search for Healing

I was told by the dog that I must take her outside to do her business. As I was leashing her, I glanced at the grandfather's clock my father built and noted, from the position of the weights, that it was not time to rewind. Perhaps tomorrow.

Then it struck me. I married and raised children. I managed a prosecutor's office. I recorded music which was sold commercially. I wrote books and magazine articles. My responsibilities are now to see that the dog doesn't pee on the floor and to assure that the clock is wound.

Last night, in the nether region between consciousness and sleep, I was aware of the cat snuggling next to my legs and, in my mind's eye, I saw the long bones of my legs, now dried and stacked anonymously in the ossuary of humanity, one more dried and wounded, broken and useless relic of a human life, and I became morose. Perhaps it is the strain of the isolation.

It was then that I thought of a story of a friend of mine. My friend had a long-time friend with whom he fell out over politics or the color of the moon or some other such nonsense. His friend came to him and extended a hand. He was leaving the area and wanted, to the extent that he could, to heal the relationship before he left. Some time after that, his friend died.

At my age, I see the ossuary of humanity with much more clarity than I do the memories which my dementia has stolen from me. I do know, though, that through my staggering, broken walk through life, there have always been people who crossed my path and gave to me the support I needed. Some of those people have left my life, with changing interests. Some have left because I was too great an ass to appreciate them. All have made incalculable contributions to the mess I call my life. It is to them that I wish to extend my hand in thanks and abject apology for any harm I have caused. Know that one old, confused and often arrogant old man is eternally grateful.

The Crux

People exist to impose meaning on existence. Life exists to deflate preposterous notions of that kind. I know. I live it. Now, I must face the consequences.

Years ago, I was taken to the doctor. I can no longer remember why, but the doctor ended up ordering a surprising number of tests which included an x-ray of my brain. On that x-ray were found the flock of black spots marking the dead areas of my brain caused by lack of blood flow. It looked rather like my having been shot in the head with bird shot. The doctors explained that each of those black spots were "dead ends", places that could no longer communicate. As it was told to me, a memory which lay on the other side of a dead end was no longer accessible unless my wondrous brain could somehow find an alternative route. The diagnosis of the doctors was "multi-infarct dementia".

The burden of this diagnosis impacted both of us. I now had an explanation for the missing memories and the difficulty I experience in navigating to places in my familiar home town. For Kathy, the diagnosis meant that she now had a husband who would require even more care. She had to drive me, for one, and she worried that I would become lost. The diagnosis was terribly hard on her. Was her husband entering upon a road which could end only with me in a nursing home and she on her own?

Time passed and I received this year an appointment with a neurologist, a Russian I had not met before. I attended the appointment. He found a relatively high functioning 75 year old. He did not refer to the x-rays nor did he look at the comments from the doctors years before. On the basis of our conversation, he announced that I did not have multi-infarct dementia. He further recommended discontinuing my meds. That turned out to be a terrible idea.

Kathy's relief was tangible. All that she had feared had been swept away in that one sentence. It was as if her life had been returned to her. I could drive myself now! I reminded her that two other doctors had made the diagnosis and she replied "When did you go to med school?" She clearly was not about to allow anything to cloud her joy.

My reaction was quite different. I've written before of my role in my family as "the smart one" and what a cruel title to impose upon a child that is. Unless I excelled at something, I could no longer be "the smart one" and that meant that I forfeited my position in the family. I could no longer be me! I had to have something to excel at to remain me!

At my time of life, I had two things: my ministry and my book. Age and illness were whittling away my congregation so the book became even more important to my sense of self-worth. Now, this one doctor is saying that the book is a fraud. I do not have multi-infarct dementia, never mind the other doctors and that terrible x-ray.

We are at the crux of the matter. Accepting the second doctor's diagnosis grants relief to Kathy, peace and contentment, but the last roar of this old lion must be filed away in my casket and deposited deep within the sod. Accepting the first doctors' diagnosis grants me permission to complete the book, to revel in the last roar of this old lion and to reclaim my sense of self-hood, but leaves Kathy with a sadness for which she never bargained.

Perhaps this will be the last chapter. Perhaps that is as it should be, in honor of life's ambiguities.